POEMS IN THE AFTERMATH

AN ANTHOLOGY
from the 2016 Presidential Transition Period

POEMS IN THE AFTERMATH

AN ANTHOLOGY
from the 2016 Presidential Transition Period

●

FEATURING

*Noah Mendez   Day Merrill   Mary Ellen Talley   Darienne Dickey
Ed Madden   Patricia Spears Jones   Risa Denenberg
Nicole Callihan   Francisco-Luis White   E. A. Gordon   Henry Israeli
James Diaz   Elaine Sexton   Jenna Le   Sergio Ortiz   Sarah Sarai
Emily Vieweg   Leah Mueller   Darius Stewart   Scott Wiggerman
Tom Daley   Veronica Golos   Sarah Dickenson Snyder
Iris Jamahl Dunkle   Anthony Cappo   Oz Hardwick   Philip F. Clark
Robert Carr   Judith Hoyer   Lydia Cortes   Joss Barton
Patricia Boomsma   Amy Gordon   J. Gay   Ina Roy-Faderman
Samara Golabuk   Lucinda Marshall   Arielle Greenberg   Lynne Viti
Vivian Wagner   Laura Winberry   Peter E. Murphy   Irene Cooper
Denise Duhamel   Suzanne Sigafoos   Charles Bernstein
Cornelius Eady   Kyle Coma-Thompson   Lonely Christopher
Joy Ladin   Elizabeth Macklin   Hilary Sideris   Julie Marie Wade
Timothy Liu   Marie Coma-Thompson   Pat Schneider   J. Bradley
Christine Stoddard   Cammy Thomas   Kristi Maxwell
Jason Schneiderman   Joanna Fuhrman   Stephanie Kaylor
Sharon Dolin   Laura McCullough   Jennifer L. Knox
Ellen Greenfield   Sharon Mesmer   Sarah Van Arsdale
Walter Holland   Denver Butson   W. P. Osborn   Lynn Schmeidler*

EDITED BY MICHAEL BRODER

© 2018 Michael Broder

Cover art: Tony Geiger (*Coronet Sunset*, 36 x 48 in, acrylic on canvas, 2016, www.tonygeiger.com)
Cover design: adam b. bohannon
Book design: Nieves Guerra-Barbazan
Book editor: J. D. Snyder

Published by Indolent Books,
an imprint of Indolent Enterprises, LLC

www.indolentbooks.com
Brooklyn, New York
ISBN: 978-1-945023-11-8

CONTENTS

Introduction: Poems in the Aftermath | Michael Broder 9

11-09-16 | Noah Mendez | Shook 13

11-10-16 | Day Merrill | Trump Wins/Clinton Concedes 15

11-11-16 | Mary Ellen Talley | Election Day 16

11-12-16 | Darienne Dickey | Chivalry Died of Unnatural Causes 17

11-13-16 | Ed Madden | 9th November 2016, The Gates 18

11-14-16 | Patricia Spears Jones | Good bourbon helps 19

11-15-16 | Risa Denenberg | When empires fail, it's always 21

11-16-16 | Nicole Callihan | Dear Gandhi— 22

11-17-16 | Francisco-Luis White | In the Mourning 23

11-18-16 | E. A. Gordon | Bomber 24

11-19-16 | Henry Israeli | Dangerous Thoughts 25

11-20-16 | James Diaz | Unnameable 26

11-21-16 | Elaine Sexton | On Rothko's "Dark Palette" 28

11-22-16 | Jenna Le | The Morning After the Election 29

11-23-16 | Sergio Ortiz | The Mind Is its Own Place 31

11-24-16 | Sarah Sarai | Beyond Reach 32

11-25-16 | Emily Vieweg | Pardon My Voice 34

11-26-16 | Leah Mueller | Seven Stages of Grief 37

11-27-16 | Darius Stewart | Dear Mr. President 39

11-28-16 | Scott Wiggerman | Aftershocks 41

11-29-16 | Tom Daley | November Shadow 42

11-30-16 | Veronica Golos | I Am a Spy in the House of Cold 43

12-01-16 | Sarah Dickenson Snyder | For Light 44

12-02-16 | Iris Jamahl Dunkle | The Map 46

12-03-16 | Anthony Cappo | Days of 2016 47

12-04-16 | Oz Hardwick | The Driver's Nightmare 48

12-05-16 | Philip F. Clark | The Emigrant 50

12-06-16 | Robert Carr | Neo-Liberal 51

12-07-16 | Judith Hoyer | When News Is Bad 52

12-08-16 | Lydia Cortes | Jetztzeit Again 53

12-09-16 | Joss Barton | Blank 55

12-10-16 | Patricia Boomsma | Arc of the Apocalypse 56

12-11-16 | Amy Gordon | Sunset 58

12-12-16 | J. Gay | 7. The Lost Penny 59

12-13-16 | Ina Roy-Faderman | digging 60

12-14-16 | Samara Golabuk | Electoral Pillage 61

12-15-16 | Lucinda Marshall | Patriotism Reconsidered 63

12-16-16 | Arielle Greenberg | Untitled 64

12-17-16 | Lynne Viti | Cyber Monday 65

12-18-16 | Vivian Wagner | Post-Election Advice From Four Poets 66

12-19-16 | Laura Winberry | #nastywoman: the anatomy of our crowns 67

12-20-16 | Peter E. Murphy | The Free Market   69

12-21-16 | Irene Cooper | No-vember   71

12-22-16 | Denise Duhamel | LETHALLY ORANGE   72

12-23-16 | Suzanne Sigafoos | Thanksgiving 2016, a Monochord   74

12-24-16 | Charles Bernstein | Were You There When
                                     They Crucified Our Lord?   75

12-25-16 | Cornelius Eady | Bad Dream   76

12-26-16 | Kyle Coma-Thompson | Tacitus Jr.   78

12-27-16 | Lonely Christopher | San Francisco   81

12-28-16 | Joy Ladin | Make America Great Again   82

12-29-16 | Elizabeth Macklin | Shanghai Mahjongg or Something   85

12-30-16 | Hilary Sideris | Real News   87

12-31-16 | Julie Marie Wade | Décima: November 8, 2016   89

01-01-17 | Timothy Liu | Ode to Barack   91

01-02-17 | Marie Coma-Thompson | Asses   93

01-03-17 | Pat Schneider | Hope Is Not a Thing   94

01-04-17 | J. Bradley | To the frog-faced men who use the word cuck
                                     as a knife   95

01-05-17 | Christine Stoddard | Thirty Pounds in Three Months   96

01-06-17 | Cammy Thomas | November 1968   98

01-07-17 | Kristi Maxwell | Before After   100

01-08-17 | Jason Schneiderman | Anger   101

01-09-17 | Joanna Fuhrman | To a New Era   109

01-10-17 | Stephanie Kaylor | On Board 110

01-11-17 | Sharon Dolin | A Momentary Stay Against Confusion 112

01-12-17 | Laura McCullough | And Also Sunflowers 113

01-13-17 | Jennifer L. Knox | A Polite Request 118

01-14-17 | Ellen Greenfield | Splitting Wood 119

01-15-17 | Sharon Mesmer | Welcome 121

01-16-17 | Sarah Van Arsdale | Ethics 124

01-17-17 | Walter Holland | The Ship of State 126

01-18-17 | Denver Butson | the aforementioned scarecrow 128

01-19-17 | W. P. Osborn | Autumn Poem 129

01-20-17 | Lynn Schmeidler | All Our Karmas Bear Fruit Without

                                    Exception 130

Contributor Notes 132

INTRODUCTION

On the night of November 8, I went to bed knowing what the outcome of the election was. We didn't sleep very well that night, my husband and I, nor did our tenants upstairs, nor most people in our Brooklyn neighborhood of Bedford-Stuyvesant, nor many people across the land. On the morning of November 9, I got up more or less as usual and sat down in front of my computer with a cup of coffee more or less as usual. But beyond that, things were anything but usual. The world had changed.

Over the course of 44 presidencies of the United States, we have had conservative presidents and liberal presidents, reactionary presidents and progressive presidents, right-wing presidents and left-wing presidents, worse presidents and better presidents. But never in the history of this nation have we had a president as unqualified to serve, on so many levels, in the most powerful office in the world, as the man to whom we woke up on November 9 as president-elect. And never have we had a president who had run on a platform so divisive, so destructive, with such little regard for the rule of law, for the land on which we live, or for the people of this nation; this nation that he said he wanted to make great again, but of the longstanding and current greatness of which he was so shockingly, if not surprisingly, unaware; this nation in whose governing principles and traditions he was so shockingly, if not surprisingly, uninterested.

I knew there would be immediate responses by artists, writers, intellectuals, and citizens, including poets. I knew that at this moment what we needed most, alongside protests and demonstrations and direct political action, was creative participation, creative responses; because the creative imagination is our most powerful tool for shaping the social imaginary, the set of ideas and beliefs that shapes our understanding of ourselves, our neighbors, and our world—natural, physical, built, social, economic, cultural, and political.

As the publisher of Indolent Books, a nonprofit poetry press that I started in 2015, I had experience with poem-a-day projects. Our HIV Here & Now project posted one poem a day by a different poet for one year leading up to 35 years of AIDS on June 5, 2016. There was another poem-a-day project on HIV Here & Now for the month leading up to World AIDS Day on December 1, 2016. I understood that a lot of people derived pleasure and comfort from those poem-a-day series. I was confident we could serve a similar role in response to the election and its aftermath, the period of the presidential transition, from the day after Election Day to the day of the inauguration.

I put out a call for submissions and had our first poem within minutes. We went on from there, soliciting poets by email, on Facebook, and via a call on Submittable. We posted a poem a day from November 9, 2016 to January 20, 2017. The call for submissions specifically took trash talking off the table. We did not want poems about orange skin or tiny hands. We did not want name-calling. We wanted poems about what we were seeing, hearing, thinking, feeling, believing, hoping and fearing in the aftermath of this stunning election. We invited submissions from poets who were celebrating as well as those who were mourning—but we didn't get a lot of those, and none ended up online or in this print anthology. We urged poets to use all the resources of poetry to engage in a rich and layered conversation about the polarization of this nation and the opportunities, such as they are, for bringing the nation and its people together, for moving forward, for making a difference.

The first poem we received was from a young trans man, Noah Mendez, who wrote about disbelief, anger, frustration, sorrow, and fear for the plight of others in even more perilous circumstances than his own ("Shook," Nov. 9, 2016). That's one of the things this election did: it gave us an opportunity to empathize, to think about the plight of the most vulnerable, to arrive at some sense of commonality through our shared precariousness. In the subsequent days, Day Merrill wrote about "the dull ache that has / replaced the frisson of terror" ("Trump Wins/Clinton Concedes," Nov. 10, 2016), while Darienne Dickey wrote about the immediately palpable backlash against the notions of equity and equality we had fostered in this country: "...he spat the blood into my face with the words / *Fucking feminist*" ("Chivalry Died of Unnatural Causes," Nov. 12, 2016).

It went on...beautiful poem after beautiful poem...for 73 days. Poets found a surprising range of vehicles for expressing their thoughts and feelings during this chaotic and frightening time: Leonard Cohen ("Good bourbon helps," Patricia Spears Jones, Nov. 14, 2016); Gandhi ("Dear Gandhi—," Nicole Callihan, Nov. 16, 2016); the tarot ("7. The Lost Penny," J. Gay, Dec. 12, 2016); Thanksgiving ("Thanksgiving 2016, a Monochord," Suzanne Sigafoos, Dec. 23, 2016); the crucifixion ("Were You There When They Crucified Our Lord?," Charles Bernstein, Dec. 24, 2016); Mahjongg ("Shanghai Mahjongg or Something," Elizabeth Macklin, Dec. 29, 2016); the 1960s ("November 1968," Cammy Thomas, Jan. 6. 2017); scarecrows ("the aforementioned scarecrow," Denver Butson, Jan. 19, 2017); and many more. I even broke some of my own rules, including a satirical poem about a *Legally Blonde* spoof by Denise Duhamel, because she of all people knows how to pull it off ("LETHALLY ORANGE," Denise Duhamel, Dec. 22, 2016).

The longest poem in this book, and perhaps the most intense, is by my husband ("Anger," Jason Schneiderman, Jan. 8, 2017). He was reluctant to let me post that poem; it was so raw. Of course, it was immediately embraced by our readership: Jason always underestimates his power to move audiences—it's the standout poem of the anthology. And believe me, I say that not because Jason is my husband; more like Jason is my husband because of the power of his poetry (and because he made me laugh 18 years ago and needed a roof over his absurdly brilliant and talented head).

The response to this project online was tremendous. The poems were avidly read and widely shared on social media. Plans were made for this print anthology. While several other anthologies have already appeared with poems written and published in the wake of the 2016 presidential election, we think there is still room for one more: *Poems in the Aftermath*; because its poems were written during the immediate post-election transition period and reflect the range of emotions that people were experiencing and that poets were capturing in their work. In fact, reading these poems now, a year or more into the Trump presidency, we have a unique opportunity for reflection—a highly particular documentation of what so many of us thought, felt, hoped, and feared in those first calamitous days. This anthology—73 poems by 73 poets originally written and posted online over the course of 73 days—lets us make a mental comparison and consider the degree of difference: then versus now. How does the reality of this presidency to date stack up against our expectations for it? Better? Worse? Or perhaps simply different? Probably all three depending on what you are considering—racism, bigotry, misogyny, homophobia, transphobia, xenophobia, immigration, the environment, trade, diplomacy, national security, the economy, taxes, healthcare; the list goes on.

In short, we suspect that this anthology remains as relevant in 2018 as it was during the transition. That's no cause for celebration, of course—a clear majority of Americans never wanted this transition to happen in the first place. Most of us wanted a different result. But we got what we got. As an entire nation, in different ways, to different extents, we did this to ourselves. And so here we are. If, as Santayana argued, those of us who cannot remember the past are condemned to repeat it, then *Poems in the Aftermath* and other books like it stand as invaluable reminders. For me, however, the questions remain: Do enough people want enough change badly enough to make it happen? Do enough people love justice enough to finally complete the bending of Dr. King's arc? Can those of us who do love justice overcome enough of our differences to work together and realize the visions of our most inspired dreamers? So much remains to be seen.

Michael Broder

Transition Poem 1 @ Nov. 9, 2016

Shook
Noah Mendez

1)
i. we all joked because it wasn't supposed to happen to us
last night i drank vodka and with cheeks red said
if trump wins i'm asking her out
cuz i'll have nothing to lose
my friends made similar bets
never thinking we'd have to cash them in

ii. i skipped my social studies class today
i couldn't sit there and hear people
cheer about last night
couldn't sit there and see people
clapping at the sight of our
nation crumbling

this is the fate of the American empire
so caught up in greed and seizing the day
that we fall under the weight
of our own ego

iii. don't bother me tonight
don't make me wake up from my dreams
you dug a grave for me
now let me lie in it

2)
i'm scared for her
she's so perfect and strong
she does nail art that could hang

in the MoMA
she's got a boisterous laugh
full of vivacity
full of love

she's not answering my texts
and i don't know her well enough to call
but she's got it worse than i
she with her masculine body
with her boyish name and
closeted feelings
weeping in the wrong bathroom for
all the right reasons

i wanted to always be there for her
when she was sad and low
but not like this
anything but this

Transition Poem 2 @ Nov. 10, 2016

Trump Wins/Clinton Concedes
Day Merrill

Trump Wins/Clinton Concedes
reads the headline of a website
I idly troll,
searching in vain for something to take
away the dull ache that has
replaced the frisson of terror,
the growing dread,
the stab of shock
of last night's election.

I conceded at 1:43 AM,
too exhausted and numb to endure
any more pundits
or statistics
or breakdowns,
other than the one I was having
on behalf of my country.

Transition Poem 3 @ Nov. 11, 2016

Election Day
Mary Ellen Talley

White pearls
around my neck
Red, white and blue pantsuit

My color scheme
is gray next day
Black pearls
around my neck

Transition Poem 4 @ Nov. 12, 2016

Chivalry Died of Unnatural Causes
Darienne Dickey

The sign read *Out of Order*
and beside it formed a line of men
inching their way instead
toward the one that read *Ladies*. Like true gentlemen,
they steered me

to the front, *Skip ahead*,
but I insisted I'd wait my turn with them because
no, I wasn't there first,
no, that's not how equality worked,
no, this is not how any of this works.

Stumbling out, still forcing the prong of his belt
back into the leather strap, he saw me,
stuck his hand out to grab my
arm and said, *Get up to the front, miss—*
interpreted me pulling away as ungrateful.

Eyes hooded by the gaud of that bright red cap,
beard swirling around his mouth like razor wire,
too close, slicing his tongue as he spoke,
and he spat the blood into my face with the words
Fucking feminist.

I watch this bright red sea ripple in celebration,
imagine it oozing from those vicious sores in his mouth.
Out of Order hangs from Liberty's torch,
yet I continue to stand in line behind men such as him
as they piss over my seat because

no, I'm not afraid of what they may leave behind.

Transition Poem 5 @ Nov. 13, 2016

9th November 2016, The Gates
Ed Madden

Bert's up early, bringing in the boxes
from last night's auction, detritus of someone's life.
He shows me a painting, a street scene somewhere
in Philadelphia, warm with autumn light.
The table lot went cheap, all art, framed things.
The yard rustles with leaves, the trees shaking
their lives off in the dark—what they've been doing
all week, roots sunk deep for what's to come.

The woman who bid against him told him she just
wanted the frames. That some of them were filled
with sketches, photos of Christo's ephemeral work
only made his story more beautiful this morning
as he told it, as he unloaded the truck, the walk
brittle and ankle-deep in dead leaves.

Transition Poem 6 @ Nov. 14, 2016

Good bourbon helps
Patricia Spears Jones

And old songs sung well
By well hung song makers
Ah Leonard Cohen, you must have been
As smooth as the bourbon on my tongue tonight
Before the moon grew larger
And sirens blasted Brooklyn's avenues
Wave after wave

On the streets of Portland, Denver, Chicago, New York
Detroit,—it feels like a Heat wave!
Combustion and courage—the ardent media watchers
Are loving the chaos they raised for ratings.

But lives are on the line. The "billionaire" and his bride
Have entered the White House
But the cameras are off
So, what will the man with the very small hands do?

Martha Reeves full throttle voice could not make any of this
Better. Not the bourbon. Or the street marching. My students
Want him gone from their vision. Funny to think that a hip grandmother
Was more preferable to the young. They know that reality tv is hard work

For seconds of edited tape. This is reel time in real time and the star
Is not equipped to deal with the real world in whatever time is real.

So best to read about a red dwarf that has haunted Detroit since 1701.
American history is full of strange ghosts that linger at corners, near
Minefields, where a bridge meets the street.

Tonight I listen to "everybody knows" and "I am your man"
And remembered why I wanted to run away to join a rock & roll band

Youthful dreams are often conventional and silly, but the man's sepulchral
Voice-bourbon, whiskey the smoke of tobacco's sweet lore. Bards are
     handsome
Are they not?

Ah, two days and we hold ourselves up against the mindful anger
Of the privileged claiming victimhood. It is vengeance they seek, not justice.
It is vengeance they shall reap—their own kind slow dancing an
     opioid ballet.
Each day a misery held by that spoon and needle routine. Dreamless.

We hear those blasting sirens vibrate the moon.

Transition Poem 7 @ Nov. 15, 2016

When empires fail, it's always
Risa Denenberg

for the greater good. Thus far, we have survived one empire after another on the enamel of the earth's teeth.

Cataclysmic events on our watch filch metric tons of gold teeth from the earth, only to enrich the affluent few.

Hordes of refugees flood fresh empires and bury children who were only begging for a crust of mud. In hopes of empires

to come, we hold foolish faith that a greater good awaits us. In this, we are probably wrong.

Perhaps the greatest good is humanity's extinction, for the good of the earth's crust, the enamel of our planet's spoils.

Empires fail. It has always been so. It could happen again on our watch. May it be for the greater good of earth.

Transition Poem 8 @ Nov. 16, 2016

Dear Gandhi—
Nicole Callihan

You should see
how hungry we've become.
Last week, I watched
a man swallow
a woman whole, on live TV,
then belch, and rub his belly.
I sing America the Beautiful
ad nauseam in my head.
Is the belly that is rubbed
contained in the same body
as a heart? Are these words
the only flag I have left to wave?

Transition Poem 9 @ Nov. 17, 2016

In the Mourning
Francisco-Luis White

Wake to another day of America, merciless with stars in her eyes. Her bosom for the free - market and white men — exposed. Her faithful court of all stripes circling her alabaster seat, desperate, abuzz. You can't help but wonder at the sight of Her about limits to redemption.

She has lied so well for so long to herself, to us and us to Her, all wanting to believe in lies older than Her name. Our deaths are sanctioned, we know. Her foot soldiers stand in blue and blood. Can't help but to hope we're at the cusp of anything but this.

Perhaps it's because she believes it's the blood of Christ she's washed in that she is forgiven, that bullets in Black backs, in Black babies are a sacrament. America's cup does run over; can't help but consider what might be incentive enough for her to change.

If not shame, or fire, or protest is persuasion it's doubtful she can be loved patiently into it. Gifts to her won't suffice, we know, as we've been taxed, long-suffered and gone without. One can't help but imagine now, the ways of doing without Her.

Transition Poem 10 @ Nov. 18, 2016

Bomber
E. A. Gordon

I was tired of trying to fit in.
And I was tired of traveling alone.

I overtipped. I cast my vote.
I was as tolerant as anyone.

Sure, I had things to say,
people to say them to,
but nothing was changing. It got worse
slowly, but one day the ground
was redder than I remembered.

What I can do is burst,
leave shavings of myself
like whittled wood
in the hands of the men who act
without me in mind.

I believe in what comes afterward,
but I keep thinking of the time
just before, when everything I was going to be
will rush forward like the cyclists
in the Tour de France,
standing on their pedals.

Transition Poem 11 @ Nov. 19, 2016

Dangerous Thoughts
Henry Israeli

Many have taken off their white shirts
and are waving them in the air. My eyebrows,
refusing to surrender, fly off like moths into the darkness.
I've come so far, I hardly have to talk
or walk anymore. Soon I'll be able to conduct
my business without leaving my bed. Still,
our very existence is endangered by one lonely rat
chewing on a wire. Turns out nothing so much as the old country
resembles the new country. Turns out there are no ghosts,
just pixelated monsters roaming our homes, our streets,
grinning, mocking, floating between us wherever we go.
It's all part of an algorithm generated in Moscow.
They tell me my love for the natural world threatens
the corporate dream of annihilation.
I've heard that the most powerful have
secret elevators that can never be found,
that don't even turn up on GPS, let alone a floor plan.
They don't need electricity because they run on
pure undiluted ego. I long for the days I was oblivious
as a dandelion. Ever since I woke up on the floor
of a vacant factory I've felt myself entangled
in radio waves. I'm scared of the government's fear of me
for where do I stand on the most important issues? I don't *stand*
for anything, and that's the point, isn't it?
It's 2016, and this is the afterlife.

Unnameable
James Diaz

For the longest time
we won't give him a name
he will be called 'That Man'
or 'This One'
like a burgeoning hurricane
we'll never know
who spotted him first
what to call
his particular danger
washing up on the shore
like poisoned letters
in a bottle
addressed to too many
vague fears
all at once

this wall was always an interior one
an impossible construction
whose fierce
overly demanding brick
I'd tear out with my soul
if I had hands
translucent enough

the hate that you store inside of yourself
can be your story for only so long
translations will shake out the fire
we'll leave buckets of water
at your door step
in the dead of night

we'll not mark our houses
we have no fear
of your angel of death
our love & resistance
will carry us so deep
into your storm
the seeds that we plant
will explode
inside of your chest

we will not give you a name
the story is ours
and our pens
are already in motion.

Transition Poem 13 @ Nov. 21, 2016

On Rothko's "Dark Palette"
Elaine Sexton

The suited guards in the gallery
usher us in. Like mourners we gauge
& weigh our pleasure
as the new climate we live in
grows grim. From this leather-
bound bench I follow the scratched
horizon crossing his canvas, cutting
pigment the color of pavement,
as our palette, our prospects to prosper
grow darker, then dim.

The Morning After the Election
Jenna Le

The morning after the election, we
converge, as usual, on the bus stop: three
commuters with no commonality
except our silent shared dependency

on public transportation. I don't know
the other two commuters' names, although
each day for weeks we've stood here in a row,
craning our necks to watch the bus's slow

climb up the skinny, frog-cold, fog-wet lane.
Overnight, something in the air has changed:
the gusts that leave the yellowed weeds deranged
now make us tremble for an unexplained

split-second longer than before. The square-
backed woman in black wool stands just a hair
more near to me than previously, to share
warmth. I smile shyly, prompting her to bare

a crescent of white teeth, though her black eyes
in her black face stay somber. To my right,
the other bus-stop regular, a light-
skinned girl with wiry spectacles and tight

glossy curls, ventures, voice soft as velour:
"You ladies think it's gonna snow?" "Not sure,"
I answer. We discuss the temperature;
the curly girl is scared she can't endure

New Hampshire's famed harsh snows: until July,
she lived in Georgia. "Moved for work," she sighs.
I give my name; "I'm Sahja," she replies.
A surge of fellow feeling warms the sky

around us three: a fragile, tender flutter.
In this new world, we must protect each other.

The Mind Is its Own Place
Sergio Ortiz

We all yearn to go back
to the edge of that fire and kick
that fucking election, the religion, the race
of an entire nation in the balls
so everything breathes
at the rhythm of our lungs.

But none of that worries us now.
We worry about the detonator of tomorrows,
the almond beyond the shell,
the shiny nugget, and the damn heat
even when we know it's November
and an eerie cold is fast approaching.

We want pleasure to surround
our waist. It can be you, or anybody else
who embraces my body
already lightened
by the burden of the world.
Yes, you can take me
to the sea inside
where there is only the sound of blood
running like a flowered beast.

And so, you go back to our room
tell yourselves,
fuck it, it's better this way?

Transition Poem 16 @ Nov. 24, 2016

Beyond Reach
Sarah Sarai

By sleight-of-hand
      her fellow
    copulator keyed   into
   a studio of sheets
and walls a matching   floral,
    a singing room from
Les Parapluies de   *Cherbourg,*
        autrefois,
  and copped a snatch of
her   warm   brain
   to sell on a green island glittery
like Dr. Moreau's.

  San Francisco nights
    in a lair
    were   squawked by
the ruffian-breed,
    half-   human blue jays,
half over the edge with   details
like frayed twine   odd strands of hair
   and   sweet grass
  scattered on sheets red
  as sky   aching that daylight
    stay and stay.

  The selling was cheap. But

the punishment nil.   Another
    saint-lost-in-ecstasy,

this woman   beyond reach of
      a million stupidities,
zip-locked against   smirks and
legalities of any too-   eager for facts.

Transition Poem 17 @ Nov. 25, 2016

Pardon My Voice
Emily Vieweg

I HAVE AN ANNOUNCEMENT

I want to fight.
I want to fight—for freedom—for myself.

What god I pray to
What higher power is to me
When life begins for me
Who judges me
Who loves me
Who wants to be
FREE.

Until the sun comes up on-a
Wash-ing-ton and nowhere else
I say what I should and should not…

I say what I should and should not…

Believe about Iraq
Believe about Iran
Believe about Afghanistan
Believe about being free.

I fight for the right to choose—what you think is best for you
So
You can fight for the right to choose—what I think is best for me.

Who wants to be free?

Though we think it's out of our meager hands
Our votes do count.
I said our votes DO count.

HA!

Our votes are counted by those that wish

to deploy our troops to "assist relations"
to instruct the beliefs of our creations
to misunderstand the nurturing of other nations.

WHO WANTS TO BE FREE?!

Mr. Bill of Rights
      Freedom of Speech
Mr. Bill of Rights
      Freedom of Press
Mr. Bill of Rights
      Freedom of Religion
            Hail Allah
            Hail Brahman
            Hail Buddha
            Hail Zeus
            Hail Athena, Poseidon, Aphrodite
            Hail Christ, Jehovah, Yahweh!
Mr. Bill of Rights.

I say FREEDOM!

What god I pray to
What higher power is to me

When life begins for me
Who judges me
Who loves me
Who wants to be—

WHO WANTS TO BE FREE!

Transition Poem 18 @ Nov. 26, 2016

Seven Stages of Grief
Leah Mueller

1). I shouldn't try
to speak to anybody:
I should just be here, where
everyone has arrived by invitation
and is on her best behavior.

2). The can has capsized,
crows pick at the remains.
Last week, the police
came to my street twice.
They made no arrests.

3). I should be here. My life
has been a series of collapses
like early airplane films. No one
is concerned, except me.
This should not
be a surprise.

4). No point in pretending
it doesn't matter. The rest is
popcorn in my movie.
The wall was always built
and waited patiently
for someone to make it visible.

5). I should be here.
End is abandonment.
The wreckage won't go quietly.

Throw my wounded shoulder
to the gate, but settle for
the opposite, until finally
everything stops working.

6). We all say
whatever we want. My
main objective is to endure
until bedtime, then repeat.
Don't forget to leave
the silverware out, in
preparation for mourning.
It saves time.

7). I never expected this knob
to last any longer
than its predecessors,
but the boss told me
it would work fine for
a few more years. I
am not responsible
for its failure, when it
finally falls apart.

Transition Poem 19 @ Nov. 27, 2016

Dear Mr. President
Darius Stewart

What will happen when there's another story
of a boy whose fate's been sealed
for a limp wrist
a lisp
a herringbone pattern
in his tie-dye t-shirt
      how will we reconcile
the senselessness we can't understand
& neither will this boy who hadn't made his bed
one morning on a whim & decided *hmmm, what if*
his pointer finger pressed to his lip
contemplating the pros & cons
but later used it to silence his blustering
to shield a purple gash so deep in the flesh
it takes weeks of healing
      what do we do when there are clues everywhere
& somehow coming in from the cold
became evidence the muddied snow-slush traipsed
over the clean carpet
the dog sniffing out the scent of another dog's shit
lingering on the boy's boot soles & *why*
how we will ask ourselves
when the roads are clear the sidewalks
clear all the way to the house a clear path
so where did all the mess come from Mr. President
will you help us
get past how dreary it's all become
to be a school-age boy in love with boys
who sacrifice *those's* & *them's* to the gods
of eternal damnation & we know why
but not *him*

this naïve lovely fool so fond of make-believe
to be a pauper or a superstar he sings to himself
as if he has a choice
as if those hallways divided
with sneers & jeers will give him a choice
as if they aren't tripping him up every chance they get
flicking their narrow fingers against his skull
barely covered with hair cause they cut it off
nicked him good in the process
that & more graffito on his locker
bitch faggot cocklicker
& there he'll be on his knees
elbow-deep in suds scrubbing away
all those *why's* & *what-did-I-do's*
wringing out rags & sponges
his grief into filthy pails you'd think it's dissolved shit
mucking up those buckets & somehow
we can't seem to do enough for this sweet boy
who sashays too much & can't sway enough souls
to his corner walking home bunched up
in that winter coat for miles shivering
trying to shake the gay away they scream at him
passing by on the school bus
hanging out windows with tongues flagging
so uncontrollably content
in their miscreant joy
they might not ever recover from it
might not ever care to see that boy again
his head bent to the wind
cinching his coat tighter
adjusting the soreness from his shoulders
each time he switches his bag from one side to the other
struggling to make it home in the cold cold
because Mr. President
all he wants is to make it
home

Transition Poem 20 @ Nov. 28, 2016

Aftershocks
Scott Wiggerman

>A golden shovel including a Dickinson last line (#799)

From some dark cavity, an affliction,
long-brooding, surfaces across America. It feels
like a brass-knuckled fist. What was impalpable

and buried has flared up and spread until
the ache of anguish is unbearable—ourselves,
our loved ones, in shrink-wrapped panic. How are
we to rise from chaos once unleashed and struck?

Transition Poem 21 @ Nov. 29, 2016

November Shadow
Tom Daley

November shadow, abide
in the tumult, in the multitude.

Let me always speak
in complete sentences
and may your long, black,
and sharpened edges keep my cool
from drying dull.

May you stretch to such a shape
that even summer will seem
a thing short and curt.

May you follow my calves
and corduroys
out the path to the place
where the tumors settle.

And may you play
your translucent black
like a splendid pack
of moles or crows.

Transition Poem 22 @ Nov. 30, 2016

I Am a Spy in the House of Cold
Veronica Golos

I am a spy in the house of cold. I nest. I tweak out the sounds a real person makes. I swallow, spit, and feed the chicks of another. How often I have felt the ice burrow, pin points of freeze upon my inner thigh, the palm of my hand. Weakness, and more. I pass. I pass through, and into, and no one knows. I am vellum, parched. I seek iridescence, but there is only the hyphen, the hajib, the gray fraying of the ends.

All is fear, and it has color. It seems a sting in the eye, a knowledge come through ghosts, gaunt, ginger man. Smack, slap, the fellowship of the hit. Help is gorgeous, it's elegance, the daffodil color at its center. I dream, always the same one. I am lost, and I am quickened by need: to find the cleansing; how do I chant its own copper sound?

There is hallelujah. Yes, somewhere inside my middle ear, the flame of it, flamingo colored, and I default, I trace in sand, plume into something else. I am ox and oyster, yes, between mouth and tongue I am. I throw my rage outward, it's neon, lunatic, a kink in the mind. Oh buffer me, I am safe in the lichen, the needled woods. I walk, and walk, and walk, and seem to never turn back. Never.

Transition Poem 23 @ Dec. 1, 2016

For Light
Sarah Dickenson Snyder

Just dip
your pen

and write,
let the words

unfurl, light the darkened
windows, the way

small candles do,
how every darkness flickers.

I will tell you about hope—when
the article I was reading in the medical library

of the Mayo Clinic in Rochester, Minnesota, gave people
diagnosed with what my father had a .05% chance of survival,

and I began to see my father as part of that spark—
how I started to watch funny movies with him in the small

hospital room to get endorphins swimming in his diseased blood,
how I made signs for this room—slogans he remembered

from the Marine Corps, *Praise the Lord—Pass the Ammo!*
Doctors nodded, saying a positive mind will help them

as they insert ports into his skull and chest to deliver poison—
how he shrunk to a skeleton as if he were melting—

many months of this, and he lived. Fifteen
more years. Let's become

cathedral builders of hope,
of listening, of a country

with a light
for each window.

Transition Poem 24 @ Dec. 2, 2016

The Map
Iris Jamahl Dunkle

The questions are slick as oil. Dive under
that dark surface, that rainbow sheen as if
there is something; espy, originate,
pioneer without a map. Facts are rock
bottom. Hit them, you'll think: pay dirt. But, facts
have cracks. California, born of earthquakes,
can't be trusted even in the solid.
When you walk from the oil your heritage
sticks to you like feathers. Dead. Promising
wind/flight/understanding.   Stories whisper
like aspen leaves: static, word, static. It's
up to you to find the narrative. And
all the while underneath: vesuvial:
that red fire that can create, or destroy.

Days of 2016
Anthony Cappo

Hushed, huddled, spinning
in the stripped wheel
             of history.

The walling of the human heart.

Pikes raised in celebration.

Sometimes the worst
                happens.

(That trembling late night call, that
      lump that turns out terminal.)

The battering ram pounds the gates,
      its steel heart taking
no questions.

Transition Poem 26 @ Dec. 4, 2016

The Driver's Nightmare
Oz Hardwick

It's the day the driver falls asleep
and seven die. You paint your face,
careful as glass, on the morning train,
and cash trickles slowly through the map's
cracks, though the news reader assures you
it'll be alright. But your house is burning
as your children sleep, and bitter letters
with no return address blister
your bloodstained fingers. You need the pills
more than ever but can't make the cost.

You strike ice behind your eyes,
while each promise is a stone you have to
swallow, 'til your veins silt, and even
cartoons clench your gut with fear,
as European rubble lays
foundations for the wall that's already there,
pens you outside yourself, and the driver
falls asleep, leaves the track,
ploughs through markets, wakes the dead,
and you're afraid of the colour of your own skin.

You are not one of those who died,
but you're sure you will be, the time bomb
hammering in your blood, as you up the volume
on the sharp suit with the razorwire grin
at the hospital gate, turning away
the burnt and twisted, counting the cash
that flutters like ashes, and you squint in the mirror,

a refugee in your own face,
and tonight the knock will sound on your door.

And as you loose the chain, the locks and bolts,
you fall asleep, leave the track,
empty pockets whistling some anthem
for which you can't remember the words,
as you hit the wall you built yourself,
peer through the door's burning crack,
appalled by your own human stink,
and brake too late, face-to-face
with your uncomprehending alien eyes.

The Emigrant
Philip F. Clark

I could not watch, had long stopped listening.
Slept—or tried; some distant place to go
in unreadable dark. We always dream,
but don't remember some. Remember
nightmares most. Countries of the mind,

these kinds of travel. My phone light
buzzes on the nightstand, or at least
it seems in my retinal miasma—I pick up,
Dublin—"Please, god, don't tell me!" Fall back,

sleep—"A dream" I think, as I bite knuckles,
grind teeth; no private Idaho. How far
and to what shore in morning or night
away from thought or action? I wake again,
shake and slough another phone buzz.

"Hell has arrived." I know.
I know, I know, I think. I know, I lift,
wash, eat, drink—I think: Copenhagen?
Nova Scotia? Christopher Street? Trafalgar Square?
Where? Here. Right here.

Transition Poem 28 @ Dec. 6, 2016

Neo-Liberal
Robert Carr

Protect private parts with a big
male hand. Imagine changing head
garb, disguising children
you don't have. Take a Xanax.

Don't speak—suck oppression
second-hand from a safe distance.
Imagine new dark days,
shirts ripped, wine bruises.

Bend for the man—under Ryan's
Reagan-blue eyes scour skin not likely
burned or flayed. His look, like yours—

water-logged. Drink wet crocodile salt,
peel leather back from a whip-welt.

When News Is Bad
Judith Hoyer

I cry behind the wheel of my car.
Little red flags flutter in my belly.
I read articles that fail to make sense of
consequences that wear black and white.
I take my brother to Herbie's
Herbie's where decisions are grilled
"A hamburger, no onion rings!"
Glad for the nearness of strangers
I wait on a folding chair to donate
O negative in a cold hall
bad lighting, kind nurses
needle pricks, tincture of iodine.
At a marquetry exhibit I fall
for a lone Great Blue Heron
whose yellow eye seems to be
searching for what to do next.
Gorgeous trees backlit by sun
middle schoolers peddling grapefruit
construction detours in our village
puncture the skin of my dysphoria.
I muster salt pork, vinegar, onions, beef
for a stew that keeps me on my feet.

Transition Poem 30 @ Dec. 8, 2016

Jetztzeit Again
Lydia Cortes

Clouds were zigzagged as if slashed
punctured with z's the z's of a sword
the sword that's mightier than mightier
sword we carry in our brain our being

in our fiber of meaning to puncture the lie
like wasps hovering near our eyes threatening
to puncture our brains our eyes and let out
all our truth that hides there in our being our

brain truth waving like a true flag of colors of
shame we're shamed into truth the truth that's
there always just behind or beyond our eyes there
but we don't we can't see most times for the fear

in our hearts covers and shields us from the truth
that we fear truly it's so loud thunderous it makes us
deaf that's the truth truth we cannot hide or bury inside
though that's what we're doing most of our lives for fear

we might get hurt might die if we uncover the truth real
blood and bile truth that comes spilling out of our brains
from behind almost right beyond our power of seeing of
feeling right under our skin's surface it's right there makes up

our fiber and muscle and bone it's there coursing in our
our veins blood truth like the lies we need to get out get rid
of the waste poisoning our lives our guts spill it out we have to
even if we bleed a bit or more we can't forever live our life's

lies we can't live forever afraid can't be forever so why
not let it all out—first comes the shit—then comes the
breath returning letting us breathe the truth life everlasting
we can't last forever but we can try to live with truth

revealed like a hallelujah busting out when we let loose
and yell like the pentacostals with tambourines singing
screaming joy engaged they're completely engaged in
the song in the sound of their body telling body's truth

truer than mere words than just sounds bursts of music
released truth dangerous truth dangerous beauty let loose
may be fatal it's bone hard bone chilling our truth the truth we
fear is now here—hear hear—and alive in us even if only for a
second for the first time—hallelujah chaos—hallelujah catharsis.

Transition Poem 31 @ Dec. 9, 2016

Blank
Joss Barton

What is a death when the life is taken by pieces
Like bricks in a stockyard instead of exploding
Like the lotto where the final jackpot is becoming
A puddle of gristle and brains to weep over
And pass laws over and elect demagogues over
And forget how wealth is always manifested
By suffering and humiliation and you smile
As if you are not complicit in this terrifying world
Of unrelenting misery but you have enough
Moral indignation to say that the system is
Broken so why not burn it all down to the sewage
Drains where the black shit water of nationalism
Saturates the air and your teeth are white like
The men whose cocks throb with every dog
Whistle calling the wolves from their caves
And their reptile cum is smeared across the
Red sambo lips of black porcelain dolls
They cradle in their arms as they draft legislation
In ink that will birth their wet American nightmares.

Arc of the Apocalypse
Patricia Boomsma

Does the arc of history bend toward justice?
Or does it just sway,
Directionless
Random
Erratic?
Does it swing like a hangman's noose in the wind
Waiting for the next martyr
Who believes her virtue will save her?

Savor the illusion of time as a willow
Weeping towards a crystal stream.
Its teardrop leaves will not heal the world.
Its broken branches fill the wide and rushing stream
That divides us, makes those on the far bank seem small
Unimportant
Foreign
Dangerous.

And see those other arcs—
Joan of Arc, an armored virgin banners flying
Blood dripping from her neck and down her leg.
Lit on fire for dressing like a man
As she waited for a just God to save her.
Or Noah's ark
Where only two of each survive
We choose our child, our friend
Our tribe the Elect.
Condemning all others
To the deluge.

I long for an Epiphany
For a bright star to follow
For Magi to enlighten me.
I stand staring at the sky
Waiting for the clouds to break
To see an arc of moon.

Transition Poem 33 @ Dec. 11, 2016

Sunset
Amy Gordon

As I stood by the oak tree, the sun moved across the sky, turning day to night. A perfect stripe of pink held my attention until three crows flew down, perched on the fence. The farmer called the sheep from pastures, the cows were called to barns. Strands of wool caught in wire knots whispered in the breeze, told me tales of olden days when women sat at home. They knitted socks for sailor men, didn't believe the earth was round. Even now, who can believe this stolid earth is round? And then the light went out. Sky hardened into blackness, the sort of black you sometimes see in the eyes of homeless men. A damp, cool hand pressed against my neck. This was the first time I had been alone under a night sky in a long time. Where were the stars? The moon? Only worms rustled in the leaves. The planet tilted, stopped, turned on its axis, reversed direction. Birds in branches above me groaned, devolving into dinosaurs. The oak tree shed its bark, a giant fern unfolded from its core, and I could smell the sea lapping up the miles on salty feet. By morning I knew I would be extinct. I began to run. How I wanted to see you one last time, and now, and now I bury my face into the lanolin scratch of your sweater. Wool is the most reassuring of all earth's gifts.

Transition Poem 34 @ Dec. 12, 2016

7. The Lost Penny
J. Gay

> From a series of poems imagining the Major Arcana
> in a modern Tarot deck

This card has seen a few revamped visual depictions, the two most popular being the sidewalk in the abandoned city and the grimy dustpan. We have chosen the sidewalk in the abandoned city, as it is both traditional and consistently relevant.

On a crumbling sidewalk next to a potted street sits a bright, burnished penny. It is accompanied by bits of paper and unidentified detritus. There are no other symbols, but the sensation of having forgotten something important, of being watched, tickles the back of your neck. Not necessarily ominous, but the copper taste of anxiety may fill your mouth and nose if you stare at the card too long.

To draw this card means nothing can be done about it. Leave it. Yes, the penny is shiny and new and you just got it as change from the store but the city is abandoned and you don't know how long the penny had been clutched in your fist when you went running into the afternoon, your eyes wide.

The reversed meaning of this card does not exist. No matter which way you look at it, no matter which direction you approach, the lost penny is the lost penny. It is not going to be found again. Leave it behind and start afresh.

Fortunate colors: Leave it.
Necessary materials: Leave it.
Ephemeral numbers: Leave it.
Lovely herbs: Leave it.
Remember: Leave it.

Transition Poem 35 @ Dec. 13, 2016

digging
Ina Roy-Faderman

white and chalky,
the skull of the world,
picked clean by
something much less than—
because you've created what's left:
a hollow bowl for bones.

this is not the work of raw-necked
vultures.
they faded with the last
long drink of water, in the dry valleys
where layers of shale
shift under the weight of sand.

surely someone warned you that blood
will be the first drink to go.
are you afraid that your sacrifice
has been for nothing?
you have sacrificed my child and
my child's children and the generations
that wither like thornapple pods
until there's
no seminal drink left, just
dry powder, with nothing left
to stir it back to life.

Transition Poem 36 @ Dec. 14, 2016

Electoral Pillage
Samara Golabuk

In the falling down of the year
and the segmentation of society,
three magical things happened:

First, we bounced on the pavement
of our vitriol, face-first into
the unapologetic wounded.

The hot wind had swept up the tumble
of love and Jesus and the old views
of cabin grandpas and alt-right housewives

who don't hate the neighbors
but sure can't stand the *negras & the gays* not
Knowing Their Place. The monsoon bivouacked

by 3am Tuesday, when hatred got a foothold
with the oligarchy's gold-lined fingerprints
and smashed up pouts, and foreheads

that chiseled fine china.
Leader of the unfree world, the world
that had its soup upturned into its face by

the monster under the bed, leaping, the one
we thought we outgrew as we Increased
into wiseness and thin-eyed generosity.

We, who never saw it coming.

Second, after the diagnosis came in,
some of us woke up choking
on our sick, dripping tears and

gasping past spasmed throats as we
tried to swallow the masses
that presented. Swing states

hovered in midair. The Age of Aquarius
ran upstream for a while.
Cats barked, and the Cubs,

having won the World Series,
ushered in a time of darkness.
They didn't mean to.

Nobody did.

Third, In the Eden of paranoia
where all the bodies are buried,
the black soil overturns itself

as if it were full of god's worms,
the turning boil of compost
rising with its heat, its chemical

burn the sprouts press through,
volunteering up into
the unremarkable sunshine,

a shockingly normal
Wednesday unlike
any other.

Transition Poem 37 @ Dec. 15, 2016

Patriotism Reconsidered
Lucinda Marshall

My anthem is the serenade of birds,
sung without regard for map lines
delineating human assumption of dominion
over that which cannot be possessed,
and I will not pledge allegiance to,
or defend a flag of illusory freedom.

As the sun greets each day,
I will bravely stand up—against
racism, gendered hate, and xenophobia.

I will join in solidarity
with those who block pipelines
and protest gun violence,
those who feed the hungry
and work to stop the school
to prison pipeline,
and with every person who works
for the common good.

Solemnly I swear not to tolerate
the revision of history to fit
a fraudulent justification for
perpetual war or
wanton destruction of Earth.

This is my oath of citizenship,
because to do anything else is treason.

Transition Poem 38 @ Dec. 16, 2016

Untitled
Arielle Greenberg

On the 78th Anniversary of Kristallnacht

while the news / came I sat in a wooden A-frame / by a creek
with my friends in their bodies / black man / trans man / black queer
    woman /
bodies blood-smeared by the president / -elect / to mark a coming /
    smiting
and we wept / I apologized / wept the bullshit useless tears of a white
    woman but /
I meant them / meant by them *I will do the work / and when they come for you /*
I will not be silent / will put my body as a shield in front of yours
and thought about how literally I might do this
(it was most like when my baby died / that sense of loss /)
and walking back in the starflung / I spoke apologies to the furious bird
who has been screaming all week
I am sorry I know I know I am sorry I said to the species
thinking of Standing Rock / then stood in more circles of bodies
then lay in bed and strategized about revolution

o fire-leveled mountain morning of noticing
in which a kind of winning, kind of conceding
has taken out my breakfast / my breath / my belief in self-evident truths

Cyber Monday
Lynne Viti

Dreams of incivility in grocery lines,
on airplanes, captive audiences of
young women, eyes downcast, heads down
while a bully in a black t-shirt castigates them.
Then a dream of riding an old two-cycle engine
Yamaha motorcycle through
a cemetery, I cruise along a gravel road
helmetless and fearless, the road
curves this way and that, till I reach
a dead end, a semicircle of half-built temples,
alabaster, deserted by masons and carpenters.
I head back, to what we still call civilization,
that made by *civis*, the citizen. My sister,
my girlfriends gather around. We feel fine,
but we've got an intestinal infection,
an orange parasitic worm. *Here,* my doctor says,
handing me a vial of pills. *Take as directed,
take with food or milk, take the full course.
Call me in three years if no improvement.*

Transition Poem 40 @ Dec. 18, 2016

Post-Election Advice From Four Poets
Vivian Wagner

Emily Dickinson whispered something
oddly capitalized and fragmented
about death and loss, before asking
if I really wanted to risk my browsing privacy by
downloading a Chrome extension that turns
Donald Trump into kittens.

Walt Whitman shouted loudly
about raindrops and universes,
waving an electronic petition
from Change.org in my face,
telling me to sign it or find myself lost.

Theodore Roethke danced drunkenly
in the corner, his beard growing out,
muttering rhetorical questions about the
existential crisis of hacking,
calling Vladimir Putin one smart motherfucker.

Mary Oliver pointed to the sunrise
with its winter pink and orange,
and then said nothing,
waiting for me to speak.

Transition Poem 41 @ Dec. 19, 2016

#nastywoman:
the anatomy of our crowns
Laura Winberry

is the smell of burning
sugar-sugar oil & sweat

we are tender
rockets burning clover
& hyssop through our abdomens

feral princesses wild & nasty
with love

all the women (in all the world)
are all the rape victims
of my dreams (in my dreams)
they sit
on the other side (of a table trying)
to explain
themselves
to a nodding
(& faceless)
man

our vaginas are not damsels in distress
they mouth the word souf with an f
& sing the triumphant blues

nasty women
licking our pre-wounds before they ooze

                              pinning up our heart-centers
                                to push our shoulders back

                                            singing the aria
                                         of dreambabydream

                                     & holding all the damaged
                                                        light

Transition Poem 42 @ Dec. 20, 2016

The Free Market
Peter E. Murphy

The Egg Lady gave birth to an egg.
The Chicken Lady gave birth to a chicken.
Although they worked in different parts
of the same industry, neither recalled

knowing the other. And, in case you're
wondering, it doesn't matter which came first.
What matters is that the young egg
and the young chicken became friends.

The egg wasn't good at getting around,
so the chicken carried it within her.
The chicken wasn't good at staying still,
so she sat on the egg and was calmed.

When the Shop Man gave birth to a shop,
he invited the chicken and the egg to move in.
Believe me, he said, You can trust me.
Believe me, he said, It's going to be great.

The Shop Man gave them space on a shelf
where the customers could see them.
Soon the chicken and the egg disappeared,
replaced by another chicken and another egg.

And on. And on.

Some people didn't notice.
Some people noticed and didn't mind.
Some people noticed and protested.

I don't know what the big deal is, said the shop owner. I am running a business. I am a for-profit business. I am not hiding from that.

And that was that.

Transition Poem 43 @ Dec. 21, 2016

No-vember
Irene Cooper

Gas station guy eyes me dead, juts me his peach fuzzed chin before back-handing my card.

Wet and dark, panhandler out Safeway says thanks, you're the first. Wears a nice Columbia fleece and good boots, easy scavenged in a ski town. I worry he looks too good, but it's poor that pisses people off.

Old showgirl leaks memory like a cracked pitcher, mourns minstrel shows with father, Young Republicans, the boiled blood of an Irish Dem mother.

Madmen and women froth with victory or grief. I'd like to excuse myself, but this is my house.

Transition Poem 44 @ Dec. 22, 2016

LETHALLY ORANGE
Denise Duhamel

"Nothing more than a Clueless redux without the edgy, knowing wit."
—The Washington Post

Lethally Orange

Donald Trump (played brilliantly by Donald Trump) has it all—hotels, golf courses, beauty pageant franchises, a reality show, a trophy wife, as well as five kids from three different marriages. But Donald wants nothing more than to be Donald Trump, the 45th president of the United States. There is one person (Hillary Clinton) trying to stop him—She is experienced. He is crass. She knows policy. He knows publicity. Spunky Donald Trump rallies all of his resources. Will he make it into the White House?

The locations for *Lethally Orange* are not, as you might have assumed, simply Florida, North Carolina, and Ohio. Although much of the film is set in such swing stages, Donald Trump (played by Donald Trump) jets to Pennsylvania, Michigan, and Wisconsin to dazzle the crowds who await him.

Lethally Orange 2: Red, White & Dumb

Donald Trump (played by Donald Trump) returns in this sequel to gloat. As he spins in his chair in the Oval Office, brassy Donald is all about rights for billionaires around the world. In fact, he puts his own luxurious vacation plans on hold as he heads to Washington, D.C., to get even more money into his pocket and the pockets of his friends. Can he also simultaneously curtail the rights of women, immigrants, minorities, and the poor? Destroy the environment? A cast of eccentrics led by Mike Pence (played by Mike Pence) quickly shows him the ways and workings, especially the loopholes, of our nation's capital.

Even though the story is set in Washington, D.C., most of the film is shot in the offices at Trump Tower in New York City or various Trump properties around the globe. The supposed "aerial views" of Washington buildings were scale models built by the crew.

Lethally Orange: The Musical

Lethally Orange is a musical with music and lyrics by Mick Mulvaney and Betsy DeVos and book by Tom Price. The story is based on the 2016 film of the same name. It tells the story of Donald Trump, a real estate mogul who decides, on a lark, to run for President of the United States. He discovers how his knowledge of the law and business can destroy others. He successfully defends antiquated, harmful views about women and minorities. In one of the most upbeat numbers, "Supporting Small Businesses," a campaigning Donald visits a small town diner and orders an LGBTQ, which he surmises is a BLT with BBQ sauce. Throughout the show, the majority of the American people have little faith in Donald Trump, complaining he is not "presidential." He continues to crush their spirits when he ignores even the most basic of civilities, his hateful tweets sung by a chorus of dancing "Trumpettes."

Transition Poem 45 @ Dec. 23, 2016

Thanksgiving 2016, a Monochord
Suzanne Sigafoos

Gathered in despair, we praised.

Transition Poem 46 @ Dec. 24, 2016

Were You There When They Crucified Our Lord?
Charles Bernstein

I was. Let me tell you about it. It was mean ugly,
disgusting. Shattering if you really want to know.
And the worst thing is it didn't stop, went on for days,
For years if truth be told. It never stopped.

Bad Dream
Cornelius Eady

It's like waking up, but not waking up
The things of this world
A film in your mouth,
Milk in the fridge a bit
Too long, you know
That flavor,

You're walking in a thrift shop
—how did you get there?
And the thought occurs
As you check the price tags
That everything you see

Once had a glory
Before the rust sat in,
Was once connected
To something bigger
Whose story

Is now gone. Forever.

Then you wake up
But you don't wake up
And you walk to a coffee shop

What happened?
Everyone there shivers and sips
Sips and shivers.

How did you all land in a coffee shop?
How come this coffee doesn't work?

The bad taste in the cup.

Transition Poem 48 @ Dec. 26, 2016

Tacitus Jr.
Kyle Coma-Thompson

His whole
autobiography
        was one
           long howl
of wounded head. So

he deserves some credit
for not writing it.

    *

Instead he surveyed the
power brokering of

the cannibal
elite, recorded them for

the sake of honesty and
moral veto. They lived

well regardless, and
passed their laws.

All so the helpless
might adhere to them.

    *

He once read somewhere
students in Australia (or
        was it

               South
                      Africa) studied
for springtime exams

under jacaranda trees in bloom,
for good   luck.

One day he would have to write
the history of the

working classes under one.

      *

They held to one
another and fought

     and cursed and kissed
     and sang their endearing

          fight songs, tumbling
          a long fall all the

way. Like blossoms. This book,

for what purpose did he write it,

but to open it one day, and catch them?

Closing it, he keeps them, safe, hidden, preserved,

indistinguishable from any other book on the table.

*

The barbarians were his people,

though they looked on him as a Roman.

Every day he conquered himself.

And so, both victor and loser, was one.

Transition Poem 49 @ Dec. 27, 2016

San Francisco
Lonely Christopher

I used to think that I could draw
and drove a car across the eclipsed
face of the thespian deserts
in a star system so far away from home
that our burning manticores fled
from the harm of a thousand space rats
and worlds died and suns were born
in a way that destroyed human concepts
of time, in a way that recalled the portal
that I once sucked ooze through
when I was first learning how to travel
and fuck for my life.

Transition Poem 50 @ Dec. 28, 2016

Make America Great Again
Joy Ladin

Put on your best shoes—
mine have holes in them—
and let's make our country great again.
I'm not talking about the election.
America has been waiting over two hundred years
to be better than its citizens,
to color outside our color lines,
to rise, once and for all
above our festering hatreds.

I'm not talking about the election.
It's time to put our ears to the ground and listen
to America rehearsing its declaration of independence
from its thirst for dammed-up rivers, its loneliness for the frogs
that are harder and harder to hear
when spring comes again—America wishes
it could stop missing them—
from the wildness of its fires, from its adolescent passions
to screw whatever it can.

I'm not talking about the election. The election
was America feeling restless, hopeless, achingly bad
about the robots running its factories
and the opiates writing its prescriptions
for how to stop hurting when you know
you will never stop hurting again,
the election was America choosing
what it never wanted
and wanting what it never had,
its hands were busy rigging its systems

to broadcast its recurring nightmares
as widely as possible
in the hopes that those of us who truly love it
will wake it up at last.

It's time for us, America's mismatched halves,
to make friends in real life, off the internet,
it's time for me to put on your shoes—
mine have holes in them—
and for us to walk, if not together,
at least in the same direction
and buy America a beer
and get teary about our childhoods
and heartbroken about our futures
until we are sure, one hundred percent,
that we will go in the morning to our different jobs
with the same throbbing in our heads.

It's hard these days to tell truth from lies,
to remember the fertility of the plains
and the sunburnt hands that work them
while riding crowded subways,
to remember the towers of tiny apartments
filled with people, old and young,
worried about paying rent
while we are logging forests we hope to God
don't have spotted owls in them.
But we all remember how to love,
and we long to be forgiven
no matter how hard
we find it to forgive,
we still watch shows whose heroes—
we still have heroes—respond to fear
with courage instead of hatred.

I sometimes remember, you do too,
to say "us" instead of "them,"
so there is no reason for either of us to fail to respond
to America's personals ad,
running on every horizon:

> Middle-aged country—
> preferred pronouns "we" and "ours"—
> seeks a few hundred million people
> who love sunrise, sunset, shining seas
> and all the land between them.
> Must be willing to shoulder two hundred years of baggage.
> Must love dogs, children, diverse eco-systems,
> a living wage for an honest day's work,
> clothing the naked, lending a hand.
> Must speak both country and city.
> Don't bother to reply
> unless you are willing to listen.

Transition Poem 51 @ Dec. 29, 2016

Shanghai Mahjongg or Something
Elizabeth Macklin

> *The living face and voice and pulse only*
> *at last hold humanity together.*
> —Walt Whitman

Let's play some Mahjongg,
let's play some Shanghai Mahjongg.
Let's play some online Shanghai Mahjongg
in our online-solitaire kaffeeklatsch,
where *Action brings good fortune,*
or can—even in Red Dragon–Hard,
one rung down from Ninja–Unbeatable.

But line 'em up. *A prayer for the post-election,*
says somebody posting a "Long Walk Home"
in the News Feed, as if to remark *Who we are,*
what we'll do, and what we won't.
And so we retreat—not into anything easy
but just into Red Dragon–Hard,
a craven occasion to try breathing.

As out in the real world they desperately try
to construe us. But we live in this one,
and wanted only to *slow down.*
A gross, 144, of pleasing tesserae: contemplation,
a way of seeing a chance—something
to do. Then doubling back to consider:
Any reason not to?

And: *Action brings good fortune!*
Or only a 68—stopped short—a joke

of the algorithm: so constantly so
it's close to a consolation. Or a passable
42, when you sense how you might've learned
something, or witnessed at last—
possibly learned.

We cannot unhear what we have heard,
says the Governor early, adding:
Protect the ship. It was as if
we could solve the problem,
here in Red Dragon–Hard,
alongside the algorithm that calls itself *I*,
placed in a bomb like an unruly child.

There are no more moves. This game is over.
You can Start a new game from the top left menu.
Here's something to do. Any reason not to?
All you have to do is know what to do
this time. Two Flowers, two Green Dragons,
and deal with the rest just a short while later.
Then it will have been done, just after that.

Transition Poem 52 @ Dec. 30, 2016

Real News
Hilary Sideris

1. A White-Tailed

single-antlered
Harlem deer

seeking a mate
in Jackie Robinson

Park is dead. The buck
became the subject

of a heated back
& forth over its fate

between our mayor
& governor.

2. Rescue Workers

shatter Suburu
windows only to find

a fake widow with roses
on her gown, blemishes

down her arm from too
much sun. Her owner,

a CPR instructor, curses
cops but goes uncharged.

The chief's relieved to
make it known that no

white woman froze in
his chic town & if one

did, his men would
notice & respond.

3. I Wondered,

said Beddal,
churchwarden

at St. Thomas of
Canterbury, why

Mr. Michael would miss
the midnight mass,

his garden decked out
as it was with Christmas

lights we could see
from the bridge.

Transition Poem 53 @ Dec. 31, 2016

Décima: November 8, 2016
Julie Marie Wade

How the weather channel describes a particularly devastating storm; Reminiscent of decimals, which we know are preceded by wholes and followed by fragments; Also, a Roman goddess of Fate; Also, a poetic form in which one four-line stanza introduces four, ten-line stanzas

Here is the beach by early light, here the gulls dragging
the sea's dark garnish across the plate of sand. Every surface
smooth as finger-tips now, mirrored, then smudged, then
picked clean again by crows. The stray voices commingling:
My cuticles have been giving me fits! and *Did you say vendors
also have to pay to be part of the showcase?* Then, this surprise
of vultures: their brown wings pulled tight as curtains, their
talons wet at the water-line. How they hunch together like monks
in common prayer. Shyly, and from some distance, I admire them,
their willingness to wait and wait for the rotted thing they want.

At lunchtime, messages blinker in my inbox. *We want your
feedback!, Quick survey to help us serve you better!,* and Sanou Bello's
missive marked as spam: *Dear friend, I hope you are fine over there in
your country.* How this greeting strangely warms me, makes me
want to inquire: *Is it Bello, like "bellow"—a scream carried on the wind—
or "bay-yo"—a handsome man?* Instead, I water the plants on the
windowsill, one moody orchid, three good-spirited ferns, and a
sober cactus. We still have not decided where to keep the beloved
cat's ashes, moved so often now, they seem to be everywhere. Later,
I type and then delete: *Dear Sanou, I cannot say if I am fine until tomorrow.*

Before Chinese takeout on TV trays, we lay supine and practice being
dead. The teacher instructs us to spread our limbs wide: *Nevermind the*

sand's small upheavals! To no good end, I picture castles made all day by children, their pails primary blue and red; then, how the tide came in, flooding their moats, drowning their turrets, and how, just now, we flattened the last of their enterprise. *Breathe.* We are playing dead but not holding our breath. When will the world ever make sense? Stars flicker like unread messages: whole galaxy pending in blind carbon copy. On each of my ten antsy fingers, the moons start to rise. What a stupid question that was: *Of course everyone pays to be part of the showcase!*

Sleep comes hurricane-rough. In the wind, I hear my own screams. Then, the world turns quiet, and I'm strolling toward Grandmother's house. Even her chimney puffs, storybook-style. In the kitchen, I find her as she always was, stoic at the sink, washing dishes. Grandma smiles, insists I wait right there. When she died, I asked my parents if she left me something, perhaps her painted shells. *Nothing*, they said. Now Grandma returns with a German shepherd, straining against the leash. *I never took him out for a walk. I regret that now, but I've been saving him, all these years, for you.* Then—I promise this is true—she tells me his name is Anger as she ties the taut loop of leather at my wrist.

.

Transition Poem 54 @ Jan. 1, 2016

Ode to Barack
Timothy Liu

When I knew
he wasn't coming

back, I didn't

wash the sheets
for over

a year, his scent

mixed with mine
until that too

became so faint

it retreated
into memory

like everything

else I had
to let go of

as I stripped

our mattress
to make room

for whomever

else might
want to

fuck me harder.

Transition Poem 55 @ Jan. 2, 2016

Asses
Marie Coma-Thompson

Magic, do as you will
and let the beaches fall
into the asses
of the people

and let the speakers
have their voices switched
for nails and high-pitched
drones

and let the rocks
fill up with water
and soften at their edges,
and I say

I will throw you.

I say

*You will be a legend to
all water
balloons*

and I say

*I'm closing my eyes now, and
let's see
who you hit*

Transition Poem 56 @ Jan. 3, 2016

Hope Is Not a Thing
Pat Schneider

God, I bow down.
I don't understand.
The world we love
strains to the point
of exhaustion.

Mercy thins, hope
is not a thing with
feathers. It is a gold
trinket in a crow's
nest, out of reach.

Teacher, teach us.
We have been here
before. The story's
end is hidden in
a cloud of future.

Our minds fail us.
Assail us, O God.
The world falls apart.
The only hope now
is the human heart.

Transition Poem 57 @ Jan. 4, 2016

To the frog-faced men who use the word cuck as a knife
J. Bradley

There is such joy when your wife tells you
how this week's stranger opened her
like a love letter, when she says "yes"
after you ask whether he left anything behind.

You can't blame her for finding men thicker than you
in all the right places. Your skin flushes
when you compare the scale of their parts to yours.

She always comes home to you.
While she sleeps, you count all the teeth marks,
bruises, and handprints. What they don't understand
is that some men need to feel small
in order to be men.

Transition Poem 58 @ Jan. 5, 2016

Thirty Pounds in Three Months
Christine Stoddard

On August 8, 2016, all 5'1 of my Salvadoran flesh and bones weighed 115 pounds.
My weight was documented, though I am myself undocumented.
This doctor accepted all patients, including ones whose parents stopped communicating with the United States Citizenship and Immigration Services when she was still in lacquered pigtails, watching *Topo Gigio* on Saturdays.
The doctor's office quoted me the same rates any documented person would pay,
but, sometimes, I still wondered if the office manager would call the police to cart me away in my hospital gown, *nalgas* flailing in the faces of passersby.
I did not harbor much trust or even hope, given that I was always second-guessing where to dock my ship next. Was it safe to live here another year without papers?
I worked for an auto repair shop, taking my weekly salary in cash, which my boss skimmed off the top from overquoted jobs that clueless customers also paid in cash.
But if my boss fired me, where would I work next? Who would hire me without my papers in order? Who would pay me as well as this seedy little business paid me every week to keep their office in as tip-top shape as I kept my ship? How would I feed my son? Would I have to return to El Salvador, which I had not seen since I still thought *Papá Noel* was real? Since I was too young to appreciate the *lorocos* in my *pupusas*? These questions were etched in my psyche, as common as asking what the weather was or if I needed to go to the grocery store. But the news made them multiply. With each tweet, each meme, each sound bite, I gained half an ounce.
I became less mobile. I sat on the sofa, hugging my son as I scrolled through my phone as a reflex. In reality, I was barely aware of his

presence. I mainly thought of him when hunger hit me. No, not hunger, simply a need for food. The election spurred my oral fixation and I had to shove whatever snack, however unappealing or unnecessary, into my mouth. He said. She said. Back and forth ad nauseam.

On September 8, 2016, all 5'1 of my Salvadoran flesh and bones weighed 125 pounds. I might have noticed if I weren't so preoccupied. Instead, I boiled more beans after work and obsessed over the latest immigration scares, as if my fear could change anything. All that changed was the fit of my clothes, especially pants.

By October 8, 2016, I had to buy new clothes as urgently as I needed to visit the doctor. That was how I found myself dialing the doctor's office from the dressing room of a discount department store. I wept as I spoke to the receptionist.

The doctor could not explain my weight gain. She only asked questions for which I had no answers. Normally, I had answers to questions, but suspected pirates would raid my ship at any moment. Surely I could not respond to "Who are you voting for?"

with "I am an illegal alien and cannot vote even though I have lived in this damn country most of my life—25 years—but that's how it is because the law is cruel."

The doctor promised to run a few tests and get back to me. I heard nothing.

By November 8, 2016, I did not recognize myself with 30 extra pounds on my frame.

My face was bloated, my hands were fat. Yet as I watched a map of the U.S. blush

until it glowed red, I knew I wasn't suffering from cancer or a thyroid condition. And I knew that it would take me four years to lose the weight,

though I might be slimming down *por allá* because of the new administration.

Transition Poem 59 @ Jan. 6, 2016

November 1968
Cammy Thomas

A reflection for November 2016

My Classics teacher at Boston University
came to class wearing a black armband.
Nixon had won, Nixon the war-monger,
the racist, the liar, had won.

The fear had started sooner, with JFK's
death, Jackie's pink, blood-stained suit,
the caisson and the riderless horse.
In Georgia, Lester Maddox threatened black people
with ax handles. In Memphis, April 1968,
King was shot dead and the cities burned,
and in June, the day after my graduation,
Bobby Kennedy was assassinated.

When that summer's Democratic Convention
turned into a riot in the streets of Chicago,
I thought the old way must end–
"The whole world is watching"–
the revolution would come and we could
exit Vietnam, cancel Wall Street, and
live in the peace of all nations.

I thought the world would right itself
and the elders give way. Instead,
George Wallace, unabashed
segregationist, won five states.

Instead, napalmed Vietnamese children
appeared in *Ramparts Magazine*,
their eyes burned off, limbs infected–
tiny amputees too sick to cry.
And that was my government.

I learned that the world kept turning
even when children were tortured.

I didn't end the war. Peace sign
around my neck, I walked barefoot
down Fifth Avenue, sang
Bob Dylan songs by heart,
read aloud from *Howl*, hitchhiked
to Arizona, to Mexico, to California.
1968 was the first time I voted,
and the bleakest, up until now.

Transition Poem 60 @ Jan. 7, 2016

Before After
Kristi Maxwell

The breadking appeared
in breaking's misspelling: his rise
accidental, and, now, yeas exchanged
for yeast. The laughability tempers
the tragedy, but does not change it.
Language always the jester.
What do you think the Cheshire cat's
grin was made of if not the word *teeth*?
But it wasn't the word, though t's
touched t's to demarcate each tooth
in the cartoon mouth. It was the idea—
and the irreconcilability between the idea
and its articulation.

Transition Poem 61 @ Jan. 8, 2017

Anger
Jason Schneiderman

When I was angry,
I kept asking how
anger works.
No one understood

my question.
Friends thought I was joking.
Or being obtuse.
Friends would say: What

do you mean
how anger works.
Anger is anger. What
are you asking.

And I would say:
Well. Is anger
a finite
material.

Is anger like hydrogen,
and there's simply
a certain amount
of it in the universe.

Is there a zero sum
of anger, a law
of the conservation
of anger,

and can we
pass it back
and forth.

Can you take my anger
and leave me less?
Can I take your anger
and then have more?

Is anger a renewable
resource, like trees
or coral reef, subject
to natural rhythms

and mass die offs,
forest fires,
and warming tides,
cycles of growth and depletion.

Is anger something
you spend like money,
that you save or spend
and is gone as it goes,

or something that
is replenished like ejaculate,
more on the way
as soon as you send some off

or is anger like ova,
each egg coming
on its own schedule,
until they run out.

Is anger like pus,
a response to a wound,
that you can drain,
or that you can heal,

or is anger like a gas
you can vent
so it won't explode
the tiny vessel

or is anger like water
that will explode
the water balloon
unless you tie it off

at the right time.
I thought someone
had to know
the answer

because I was consumed
by anger,
it was under
everything I did

I felt it all the time,
all the time,
and it never
departed.

I didn't have a breakdown,
though I asked friends
if what I was experiencing
was a breakdown (no,

they said, a breakdown
looks only
like a breakdown), and
I looked OK,

but no one knew
how to help me,
and I told a friend
that I wasn't OK

and she told me
that I was OK,
but the anger was there
all the time,

like a pair of shoes
that were always
between me
and the ground I walked on,

and I kept asking everyone
how anger works:
Can you drain it?
Can you vent it?

Can you stop it?
Can you heal it?
Can you trade it?
Can you sell it?

And no one,
no one, no one,
no one knew
what I was asking

until finally
someone asked me
to describe
what I was feeling,

and she said
you're not talking
about anger
you're talking about rage,

and I realized
that I've never
experienced anger.
I only know rage.

Which helped a lot.
Which explained why
I could only think
about striking out

and then not strike out.
Which explained why
I knew which plants
in my garden could be made

into poisons, and how.
Which explained
why my daydreams
turned into

elaborate fantasies
about harming people,
until I did the things
I imagined to myself,

and listen, please listen,
I knew it was bad,
and I wanted out, but
I couldn't write

my way out of it,
and I couldn't think
my way out of it,
and I couldn't love

my way out of it,
and I couldn't read
my way out of it,
and I thought I would live

with it forever,
that I would contain
it at whatever price
I had to pay,

and I'm telling you this,
and I need you to listen,
because I'm saying
that I do understand

what it's like to want
everyone else to suffer
as much as you
are suffering,

and I understand
what it's like
to want to die
both to contain

the pain of rage,
and to spread
the pain of rage,
and when you read

of this murder or
that bombing, know,
these killers are not
inhuman or monstrous,

but rather that they
are weak vessels for rage,
that they are balloons
that burst with their rage,

that they are pipe bombs made
of flesh and bone,
and peace is what I want
more than anything else,

but peace is so fragile,
so easy to take, so easy
to lose, and so they take it
from you, to feel less alone,

and I'm out of it now
because I thought
I had done it to myself,
but I didn't. And I see

that now. I'm closer
to peace. I'm further

from rage. I'm a bomb
no longer ticking,

but I was a bomb.
Hold me tight.
I was a bomb.
Hold me tight.

Transition Poem 62 @ Jan. 9, 2017

To a New Era
Joanna Fuhrman

Fuck you with your tufts of violence
growing above your groin
with your busted lip called media
and your automatic, gilded
imitation-platinum blade-studded cock ring,
encircling a planet you're ready to destroy.

The Old Era may have been a fragment
floating in an ocean of private prisons,
chicken-shit rivers, and remote
controlled wars, but it smelled like lilacs
and artistically-sourced lattes
and it knew how to read on a 12th grade level.

Unlike you who reduces Wollstonecraft's
Vindication of the Rights of Women
to a garbled idiom tattooed in micro-script
above Frankenstein's monster's blazing pee-hole.

Please, gods of sunlight and morning naps,
goddesses of semicolons, give us
another chance to welcome in
the better angels of nurture,

to open our arms wide enough that our flesh
becomes a stained-glass house
the exile can find comfort in and recreate
out of whispers and tulip hearts.

Let our desire for kindness be larger
than the sickness of our fear.

Transition Poem 63 @ Jan. 10, 2017

On Board
Stephanie Kaylor

truck: commodities for bart-
er or exchange, etymologically
preexisting the engine, its
oil & mechanics only incidental
((bearing no weight no name
but that which was waiting at
the loading dock
like a virgin womb
finding itself taken
onboard))

***

in Pennsylvania
the men were always
real men   waiting
was the road between
here
and there

on the horizon
a woman in diamonds,
the lipsticked outline
of a sun setting into No

***

a girl waits
at the truck stop

where she heard her life
will be great

again
in the passenger's seat
of a vehicle made for one
solitary driver sweating

his crumpled bills still
warm in her faux leather
purse, he told her
afterward she owed him
change

pants around his ankles

a withering erection
pointing toward god

Transition Poem 64 @ Jan. 11, 2017

A Momentary Stay Against Confusion
Sharon Dolin

Why not prolonged confusion
        against a momentary stay

or a momentary confusion
        against a longer stay

why not a momentary lay
        against contusion

why choose clarity
        over confusion

and the moment over
        the continuing confusion of

every world's stay

and why *against*
        instead of *for*

a momentary stay for
        confusion

confusing moments
        for the staying.

Transition Poem 65 @ Jan. 12, 2017

And Also Sunflowers
Laura McCullough

Distracting myself, I discover the year 1510,
an interesting one, recall the old Chinese curse:
May you live in interesting times. The election

turned, and it was only you I wanted
      to talk to, but you'd changed the way you'd voted
about our marriage. My grown son called;

white and with guns, he said, "The revolution
is coming, and I'll protect you," but knowing
the different triggers we'd each pulled that day

only made me feel lost in the maze of our loves' histories.
      My private civilization seemed
twisted, every passage a dead end, and the morning

after, people walked looking down as if distrusting
even their own feet, and I felt strange community
in our grief. No wonder I am looking back

at other times. That week, the unearthed skeletons
of a mother and baby lain precisely
      on a spread swan's wing made me weep

because you aren't here. I can only describe
the feathered gesture in the six thousand year old grave
      as majestic though the word for *elegance*

wouldn't be invented until 1510. Also that year,

England's Henry VIII was 18, a boy-man with a world
      of violence yet to manifest in his future,

the Portuguese General Albuquerque,
      Christian empire builder, would conquer part of India
for the spices—black pepper, cinnamon, cardamom—

calling it *trade*, and the 10th emperor of the Ming Dynasty
would defeat a rebellion involving a prince, a eunuch,
      and the perennial issue of tax reform.   Oh,

in that year, a random one, so much occurred, and this, too:
      the first pocket watch was built in Germany.
I am trying hard to think about time, how it grows,

collapses in moments of loss or betrayal, our fascination
      with the gears of humanity, how one person's future
is another's past, one culture's colonization is another's "settling".

      Yesterday, in a public space, a woman admired my ring,
then crossed the borders of our bodies to touch my bare arm
      with such tenderness of invasion that my throat

loosened and the hairs on my neck
      shivered like feathers riffling.   I almost felt
unafraid.   Later, at twilight, my neighbor once

again shooing deer from his untended shrubs,
      arms overhead, looked as if he were being
chased by something terrible and dangerous.

      My son may have wanted to make me feel safe.
      My husband may feel shame and guilt alone
in his rented hut.   I take everything in so personally.

My life is interesting, and I feel cursed,
though there is no such thing as that "Chinese curse".
      The phrase was popularized when Robert Kennedy

used it in his "Day of Affirmation Speech" in 1966
at the University of Cape Town, South Africa.
It came first from the English ambassador to China

in his 1949 memoir.
      It may have come from this expression:
"寧為太平犬，莫做亂離人"

    (nìng wéi tàipíng quǎn, mò zuò luàn lí rén)
which I read is translated as
Better to be a dog in a peaceful time,

    than a human in a warring one,
but when I tried to verify this myself
in Google Translate I got: *For the Pacific dog,*

    do not leave people from chaos,
so surreal, it feels right right now.   Turning back
      to 1510, it turns out sunflowers are American,

cultivated by the First People's of New Mexico
and Arizona.   Spanish explorers brought them
      to Europe, and then they were cultivated in Russia,

and in 1887, late in a Paris summer, Van Gogh
painted four canvases with rings of yellow
      feathery leaves around seed-heart discs, seeds

that, ground or pounded into flour, make
cakes and bread, and I've read the pulped
      roots can even draw poison from a snakebite.

It was the Italians who patented, in 1716, squeezing
          the seeds for oil, and today, the biggest fields
are found in Tuscany and described as endless. Closer

          to home, in the New Jersey farmlands most people
don't know exist, one can get lost in a sunflower maze
          at Liberty Farm for just $10 per adult, $6 for kids,

though a recent sign—No Drones Please—
seems so complicatedly American. Bobby Kennedy's speech
          in South Africa is also called

"The Ripple of Hope" and he spoke against apartheid,
and for the effect of individual efforts:

A young monk began the Protestant Reformation, a young general extended an empire from Macedonia to the borders of the earth, and a young woman reclaimed the territory of France. It was a young Italian explorer who discovered the New World, and 32 year old Thomas Jefferson who proclaimed that all men are created equal.

All males, yes, and the unexamined issues of classism, racism, sexism,
          were only beginning to be seen as poisons
needing antidotes,
                    and I was just eight

when a young Palestinian man shot and killed him,
the train with his body going from Boston to DC,
my family and me standing in a string of knots,

our community of Irish and Italians and Poles lined
along the tracks in Merrill Park, the women crying,
and whispering "Not another one."
                              Was it the year

I became politically conscious? Began to wonder
about the ways we are connected? I had not
heard nor read:

It is from numberless diverse acts of courage and belief that human history is shaped. Each time a [person] stands up for an ideal or acts to improve the lot of others or strikes out against injustice, [s/h]e sends forth a tiny **ripple of hope**, *and crossing each other from a million different centers of energy and daring, those ripples build a current that can sweep down the mightiest wall of oppression and resistance.*

Nor had I seen Van Gogh's sunflowers, all those blind eyes,
nor understood the seed head pattern
is Fibonacci, named after the Italian who used

the discovery by the poet Virahanka living in India
in the 6th century.
                              I don't understand
      math, but that doesn't stop me from *feeling*

as I look at the whirled flowers, paint strokes for seeds
      a pattern discovered and then explained
by people on different continents,
                              but I can see

the fallen petals of family, community, and country
as exposing patterns so complex and embedded in time—
the many futures of so many people's pasts—that I am both

awed by the elegance and terrified of what will come
to pass, feeling alone and hopeless but trying to believe
in one thing: time, both endless and terminal.

Transition Poem 66 @ Jan. 13, 2017

A Polite Request
Jennifer L. Knox

"They answered!" Stan yipped and tilted the phone so I could hear: crackly static (we knew it would be). We waited ages for the beep, then Stan recited the script, calm as balm, all blame and rage scoured from his voice: "By sheer luck we are not ones underground, but we hear the tunneling. We put the money in a bag made of yodels like you like it and gave it to the eagle on top of our flagpole. It's in his talons till you need it. Happy birthday," Stan said, then gingerly closed the flip phone in a fluid Kung Fu move. Once he'd have slapped it shut like a castanet, but now—who knew how long anything needed to last. "You're so good at that—I'd just cry," I said, ashamed. "Don't you dare," Stan warned, so, of course, I did, so the phone started ringing, then the doorbell: more phone numbers—my hands, stained clown red from the China marker nub I'd been scrawling them on walls with. Then I saw the black limousine go by again—still circling for days now. So close I could touch it. The tires, at least. "Do we still have that box of carpet tacks?"

Transition Poem 67 @ Jan. 14, 2017

Splitting Wood
Ellen Greenfield

Here in the chill November light
My job is splitting wood for winter.
True, I am too small of stature
To wield an axe
But I can use a different tool.
True, I have to plug it in
But it transforms little power into great strength.

Looking at the space the wood must fill
I almost despair –
So much emptiness to address
But I can start.
I choose a heap of logs to split
Then run them one by one through the splitter.

Each demands my scrutiny:
How does the grain flow? Where are the knots?
I nestle one in the cradle
And press a switch to trigger the chassis –
Five tons of hydraulic pressure
Conveys the wood, unyielding, toward an immoveable wedge.

Some crack easily, others resist:
The toughest snap back to slam a leg
Or mash a finger.
But soon another pile grows –
Logs readied for the fire.
These I pitch into the barrow and wheel to the porch
(An awkward load and hard to balance)

Where I stack them, armload by armload
Close at hand, to last through winter.

From pile to splitter
        Splitter to pile
                Pile to barrow
                        Barrow to porch
Armload by armload.

And when I take stock again,
The waiting space is almost filled
The work is getting done
Winter's bitterness will be overcome.

Transition Poem 68 @ Jan. 15, 2017

Welcome
Sharon Mesmer

*A student asked, "When times of great difficulty visit us,
how should we meet them?"
The teacher said, "Welcome."*
— Buddhist saying

Welcome subsiding of light
Welcome turning of the year

Welcome unexpected conclusion

Welcome abyss divulging its form

Welcome darkness that is another sun

Welcome all we are about to lose
Welcome all we are about to gain

Welcome sitting with all that is difficult

Welcome climbing the ladder of the spine
and drinking the breath in in a single sip

Welcome no thoughts

Welcome many thoughts

Welcome wound that never heals

Welcome event horizon where familiar things disappear

Welcome age of chaos

Welcome carefully choosing words so as to not tell everything because certain things lose fragrance in air

Welcome loss of words — in a little while
there may be many

Welcome no words

Welcome many words

Welcome all that is difficult

Welcome all-consuming weariness

Welcome familiar joys tinged with bitterness

Welcome reversal

Welcome moment when something new appears
Welcome unknown frontier that forces us to become
more than we ever were before

Welcome all that is difficult

Welcome turning all mishaps into the path
Welcome driving all blames into one
Welcome being grateful to everyone

Welcome new poem that some will dismiss
Welcome new poem that some may misunderstand

Welcome new poem written quickly wherein I say
"Welcome, new future of which I am not afraid

for I have already looked into the abyss
and am prepared for light"

Welcome subsiding of light

Welcome returning of light

Welcome turning

Turning, turning

To light

Transition Poem 69 @ Jan. 16, 2017

Ethics
Sarah Van Arsdale

In a future I cannot imagine
will we say to each other,
remember that afternoon,
that thing with the ethics committee,
that *was when everything changed?*

Will we say,
was that before the inauguration,
and puzzle it out, tethering from Christmas
to Joan's party the day after New Year's Day

yes, it was early in January
yes, it was between the election
and the inauguration

Will we say,
remember, we drove up to the Catskills
it was raining
and we stopped for gas
and I bought a Times *because the headline*
was so alarming

and we kept driving north on the Taconic
and it was that stasis
between late fall and true winter:
raining, but just after Hopewell Junction
the pond that forms there between the northbound
and the southbound lanes
was frozen over with a skin of ice

and the desperate trees, bare of leaves
scratched against the fog-heavy sky
and the apron of woods
banking up from the parkway
lay littered with leaf meal
and patches of early snow.

Will we remember this afternoon,
the rain, the *Times* tossed into the back seat,
arriving at last, the clumps of snow
heaped by the trunks of the trees,
the warm purr of the furnace,
the roses resting, wrapped
against the coming freeze?

Transition Poem 70 @ Jan. 17, 2017

The Ship of State
Walter Holland

changes course,
doors swing right and left unhinged
and on a dark sea and in a dark room

the engines come to a halt. Slowly
lights go out, one by one
shimmer and die

while faint voices sound
alarm and huddled on the top
deck, the men in tuxedos

women adorned, chatter on;
a pause in the music,
a respite from the dance

a tinkling of crystal
while the great silence below ensues
where immigrants in steerage

cower on half-knees and
in the vast hull of the ship
the water seeps in

to the cries of workmen
soaked in sweat. A captain
half-distracted, half-amused

calls from his tower room,
as the ship begins to list,
his assistants bark their orders

with absurd futility;
they argue about the chain of
command, their loyalty

and then the creak of iron,
to stairways thronged, the half-awake
driven from their sleep

wait to climb to higher ground;
and the compass merely spins,
as the great bow plunges down.

the aforementioned scarecrow
Denver Butson

is not holding his head down because it is autumn and because the weight of the year has weakened him. he is not bent over because it is time to acquiesce to gravity at last. he is not disintegrating into himself as is the custom of scarecrows come October come November. the aforementioned scarecrow is not simply doing what scarecrows have always done and dissolving when the days grow short and dark comes fast. no. the aforementioned scarecrow is weeping like he has never wept before. angry like he has never been angry before. and he is gathering his sadness and his rage into power he has never known before. the aforementioned scarecrow is mustering up all his straw and mud and crumpled paper and dust. to lift his head for once in his long life of standing still. and to scare the falling sun from falling. and if not that to scare the fallen sun to pull itself back up and rise again.

Transition Poem 72 @ Jan. 19, 2017

Autumn Poem
W. P. Osborn

A gap between the eave and roof showed smoke.
I went to look; perceived an attic flame.
Emergency: Your help is on the way.
Just time to get the cats into their cage
and listen for a distant siren's wail.
It didn't come; my lungs could draw no air.
I phoned again; the woman said she'd failed,
would send a rig to help without delay.
The smoke grew thick, the flames consuming all,
blue and orange flaring through the eaves
and seeping out the downstairs window frames.
I smelled it now, the stink of tires and leaves.
I heard the wind roar; fire makes that sound.
I dreamed our little house was burning down.

Transition Poem 73 @ Jan. 20, 2017

All Our Karmas Bear Fruit Without Exception
Lynn Schmeidler

Nobody saw it coming but the florist whose data—
she loves me she loves me not—presupposed the peaceful
transfer of affection. Despite the heart in my cris de coeur,

elections are not love songs. I come from the country of
what happens to me happens to you. We might have coupled
on a ballroom floor strewn with ceiling shards

in the bed-ridden monopoly of a moment in herstory,
but we refused to consider the desire of pavement
to crack. We might have recited The Book of Shadows

or broken flesh with one another in a ritual
of witches had there been more play in our defeat. As it is,
one more binge of fatal choices and I might split open

in a gutted mess of slogans at the profane communion table
of a felled future. America, bikini-craving brain
doused in dopamine, when it comes to a free vacation

giveaway where wine is spilled on promiscuous lips,
you're an easy mark. With each exhale let go of your
attachments, one by one. We might have given birth to a butterfly,

fed a forest at our breast, lived and been counted. Once,
I was swaddled in footed pajamas, now tomorrow
comes up as unavailable on my caller ID.

And what's with the daily news, breaking like a rogue wave
over the ocean liner of my guided meditation?
Hope has a shyster's face printed in blood on its wings.

I hold out my begging bowl to this new now.

Editor's Note: This poem includes in its entirety Mina Loy's "Love Songs to Joannes," section III, which is in the public domain and reads as follows:

We might have coupled
In the bed-ridden monopoly of a moment
Or broken flesh with one another
At the profane communion table
Where wine is spilled on promiscuous lips

We might have given birth to a butterfly
With the daily news
Printed in blood on its wings

CONTRIBUTOR NOTES

Joss Barton's work has appeared in *HIV Here & Now*, *Ethica Press*, *Vice Magazine*, and *Vetch Poetry: A Transgender Poetry Journal*. She is a writer, photographer, journalist, and artist documenting queer and trans* life and love in St. Louis. In 2016 she was a member of the first ever Summer Trans Women Writers' Workshop, co-sponsored by *Topside Press* and Brooklyn College. She was a 2013 Fiction Fellow at the Lambda Literary Foundation's "Emerging LGBT Writers Retreat", and a contributing artist for Nine Network's "Public Media Commons Artist Showcase" in 2015. She is an alumna of the Regional Arts Commission's Community Arts Training Institute.

Charles Bernstein is the author of *Pitch of Poetry* (University of Chicago Press, 2016), *Recalculating* (University of Chicago Press, 2013), *All the Whiskey in Heaven* (Farrar, Straus, and Giroux, 2010), and *Girly Man* (University of Chicago Press, 2006). He is Donald T. Regan Professor of English and Comparative Literature at the University of Pennsylvania, where he is co-director of PennSound.

Patricia Boomsma's poems, stories, and reviews have appeared in *New Orleans Review*, *Scarlet Leaf Review*, *Vignette Review*, *Haiku Journal*, and *Persimmon Tree*. Her work received an honorable mention in the 2016, and an outstanding haiku award in the 2017, haiku contests of the Arizona Matsuri festival. She is a recent MFA graduate from Queens University of Charlotte, where she was an editorial assistant for *Qu* magazine. She is also an Arizona lawyer.

J. Bradley's books include *Dodging Traffic* (Ampersand Books, 2009), *Bodies Made of Smoke* (HOUSEFIRE, 2012), *The Bones of Us* (YesYes Books, 2014, illustrated by Adam Scott Mazer), *It Is A Wild Swing Of A Knife* (Choose the Sword Press, 2015), *No More Stories About The*

Moon (Lucky Bastard Press, 2016), *The Adventures of Jesus Christ, Boy Detective* (Pelekinesis, 2016), and *Pick How You Will Revise A Memory* (Robocup Press, 2016). His chapbook *Neil* (Five Quarterly, 2015) won Five Quarterly's 2015 e-chapbook contest for fiction. He received an MFA in writing from Lindenwood University.

Denver Butson is the author of *triptych* (The Commoner Press, 1999), *Mechanical Birds* (St. Andrews College Press, 2001), *illegible address* (Luquer Street Press, 2004), and *the sum of uncountable things* (Deadly Chaps Press, 2015). His work has appeared in anthologies edited by Billy Collins, Garrison Keillor, and Agha Shahid Ali. He has been regularly featured on NPR's Writers Almanac and has earned an individual artist fellowship from the New York Foundation for the Arts. He has collaborated with several artists, including Mat Maneri, Marco Cappelli, Maria Mercedes Martinez, and Pietro Costa. He lives with his wife, actress Rhonda Keyser, and their daughter Maybelle in Carroll Gardens.

Nicole Callihan is the author of *SuperLoop* (Sock Monkey Press, 2014), *The Deeply Flawed Human* (Deadly Chaps Press, 2016), *Downtown* (Finishing Line Press, 2017), and *Translucence* (Indolent Books, 2018), an English-Arabic collaboration with Palestinian poet Samar Abdel Jabar. She is the co-author of *Henry River Mill Village* (Arcadia Publishing, 2012, co-author Ruby Young Keller), and the 2015 Baltic Writing Residency Chapbook Contest winner *A Study in Spring* (Rabbit Catastrophe Press, 2015, co-author Zoë Ryder White). Her poems have appeared in *PANK, Painted Bride Quarterly, PEN America*, and as a Poem-a-Day for the Academy of American Poets.

Anthony Cappo is the author of the chapbook *My Bedside Radio* (Deadly Chaps Press, 2016). His poems have appeared in *Prelude, Connotation Press: An Online Artifact, Pine Hills Review, Yes Poetry, The Boiler*, and other publications. He received his MFA in creative writing from Sarah Lawrence College. He lives in New York City.

Robert Carr is the author of *Amaranth* (Indolent Books, 2016). His work has recently appeared in *Bellevue Literary Review, Kettle Blue*

Review, New Verse News, Radius Literary Magazine, Pretty Owl Poetry, White Stag Journal, The Good Men Project, and other publications. He serves as deputy director for the Bureau of Infectious Disease and Laboratory Sciences with the Massachusetts Department of Public Health. He lives with his husband Stephen in Malden, Massachusetts.

Lonely Christopher is the author of the poetry collections *Death & Disaster Series* (Monk Books, 2014) and *The Resignation* (Roof Books, 2018), the short story collection *The Mechanics of Homosexual Intercourse* (Akashic Books, 2011), and the novel *THERE* (Kristiania, 2017). He also writes for stage and screen and lives in Brooklyn.

Philip F. Clark is the author of *The Carnival of Affection* (Sibling Rivalry Press, 2017). His poems have appeared in *Assaracus Journal, The Good Men Project, The Conversant, HIV Here & Now,* and other publications. He reviews poetry for *Lambda Literary Review*. He is an adjunct lecturer in English and poetry at City College, NYC, where in 2016 he received his MFA in creative writing.

Kyle Coma-Thompson is the author of the short story collections *The Lucky Body* (Dock Street Press, 2014) and *Night in the Sun* (Dock Street Press, 2016). The title story for his first book was included by Ben Marcus in the anthology *New American Stories* (Vintage, 2015). His work has appeared in *The White Review, Full Stop Magazine, Conjunctions, Electric Literature,* and other publications. He lives in Louisville, KY.

Marie Coma-Thompson's work has appeared in *Maudlin House*. She has been a featured reader at the Speak Social reading series as well as a featured emerging writer at the InKY series. She lives in Louisville, KY where she teaches Kundalini Yoga and attends graduate school for clinical mental health counseling.

Irene Cooper's poetry has appeared in *The Feminist Wire* and has been published in *Verseweavers* (Oregon Poetry Association, 2016). She holds an MFA in poetry from Oregon State University-Cascades, and co-runs the blog *(Eternal) Beginner's Guide to Bend* with Laura Winberry. She writes, teaches, and lives in Oregon.

Lydia Cortes is the author of *Lust for Lust* (Ten Pell Books, 2002) and *Whose Place* (Straw Gate Books, 2009). Her work has appeared in various anthologies, online zines, and literary journals, including *upstreet*, *The Anthology of Puerto Rican Poetry: From Aboriginal to Contemporary Times* (University of Massachusetts Press, 2006), *Through the Kitchen Window* (Bloomsbury Academic, 2006), and *Breaking Ground: Anthology of Puerto Rican Women Writers in New York 1980-2012* (Editorial Campana, 2012). She is currently working on a memoir in verse form.

Tom Daley is the author of *House You Cannot Reach—Poems in the Voice of My Mother and Other Poems* (FutureCycle Press, 2015). Recipient of the Dana Award in Poetry, his poems have appeared in *Harvard Review*, *The Massachusetts Review, Fence, Denver Quarterly, Crazyhorse, Witness*, and other publications. He leads writing workshops in the Boston area and online for poets and writers working in creative prose.

Risa Denenberg is the author of *Whirlwind @ Lesbos* (Headmistress Press, 2016). She is a nurse practitioner working in end-of-life care. She reviews poetry for the *American Journal of Nursing* and is an editor at Headmistress Press, a publisher of lesbian poetry. Her collection *Slight Faith* is forthcoming in 2018 from MoonPath Press. She lives on the Olympic Peninsula in Washington.

James Diaz is the author of *This Someone I Call Stranger* (Indolent Books, 2018). His work has appeared in *ditch,, Chronogram, CHEAP POP, Foliate Oak Literary Magazine, The Voices Project, Pismire, Epigraph Magazine, My Favorite Bullet, The Kitchen Poet, Degenerate Literature, Collective Exile*, and other publications. He is the founding editor of the literary arts magazine *Anti-Heroin Chic*. Both poet and activist, he lives in Upstate New York.

Darienne Dickey's work has appeared in *HIV Here & Now, The Eckleburg Project, The Albion Review*, and *Firewords Quarterly*. She works as an editorial assistant for *Callaloo,* a literary and academic journal of African Diaspora arts and letters, and as an assistant editor for *Bartleby Snopes*. She is an alumna of Texas A&M University's Black Box Writers Residency, where she received her BA in creative writing, and was awarded the 2016 Charles Gordone Award for Undergraduate Poetry.

Sharon Dolin is the author of six poetry collections: *Manual for Living* (University of Pittsburgh Press, 2016), *Serious Pink* (Marsh Hawk Press, 2015), *Whirlwind* (Pittsburgh, 2012), *Burn and Dodge* (Pittsburgh, 2008, winner of the 2007 AWP Donald Hall Prize for Poetry), *Realm of the Possible* (Four Way Books, 2004), and *Heart Work* (Sheep Meadow Press, 1995). Among her awards are a 2016 PEN/Heim Translation Fund grant, a 2013 Witter Bynner Fellowship, and a Pushcart Prize. She directs and teaches in Writing About Art in Barcelona each June.

Denise Duhamel is the author of *Scald* (University of Pittsburgh Press, 2017), *Blowout* (Pittsburgh, 2013, finalist for the National Book Critics Circle Award), *Ka-Ching!* (Pittsburgh, 2009), *Two and Two* (Pittsburgh, 2005), *Mille et un Sentiments* (Firewheel, 2005) and *Queen for a Day: Selected and New Poems* (Pittsburgh, 2001). A recipient of awards from the National Endowment for the Arts and the Guggenheim Foundation, she was the guest editor for *The Best American Poetry 2013*.

Iris Jamahl Dunkle is the author of *There's a Ghost in this Machine of Air* (Word Tech Editions, 2015) and *Interrupted Geographies* (Trio House Press, 2017). Her first poetry collection, *Gold Passage* (Trio House Press, 2012), was selected by Ross Gay for the 2012 Trio Award. Her chapbooks include *Inheritance* (Finishing Line Press, 2010) and *The Flying Trolley* (Finishing Line Press, 2013). Her poetry, essays, and creative nonfiction have appeared in *Fence, Calyx, Catamaran, 2013 Poet's Market* (Writer's Digest Books, twenty-sixth edition, 2012), *Chicago Quarterly Review*, and other publications. She teaches writing and literature at Napa Valley College and is on the staff of the Napa Valley Writers conference. She currently resides with her family in Northern California and is the 2016-2017 Poet Laureate of Sonoma County, CA.

Cornelius Eady, cofounder of Cave Canem, is the author of more than half a dozen volumes of poetry, among them *Victims of the Latest Dance Craze* (Ommation Press, 1985, winner of the Lamont Poetry Prize from the Academy of American Poets), *The Gathering of My Name* (Carnegie Mellon Poetry Series, 1991, nominated for a Pulitzer Prize), *Brutal Imagination* (G.P. Putnam's Sons, 2001, a National Book Award finalist), and *Hardheaded Weather: New and Selected Poems* (G.P. Putnam's Sons, 2008).

Joanna Fuhrman is the author of five books of poetry, most recently *The Year of Yellow Butterflies* (Hanging Loose Press, 2015) and *Pageant* (Alice James Books, 2009). Her poems have appeared in many journals, including *New American Writing, The Believer, Volt, Fence, Lit, Quarterly West*, and *Conduit*. She teaches poetry writing at Rutgers University, and in public schools through Teachers & Writers Collaborative and Sarah Lawrence College's "Writer's Village".

J. Gay is the author of *Decomposition* (dancing girl press, 2014). Her work can be found on *wicked alice* and in the anthology *Pop Fic Review* (Underwords, 2011). She's an alumna of the College of Santa Fe and received her MFA from Stonecoast. She was born in Louisiana and now lives in New Mexico.

Samara Golabuk's work has appeared or is forthcoming in *Strong Verse, The Whistling Fire, Inklette, Peacock Journal, Memoryhouse Magazine, Razor*, and other publications. She is a two-time Pushcart Prize nominee. She has two children, works in marketing, has returned to university, and will complete her BA in poetry in the summer of 2018.

Veronica Golos is the author of *A Bell Buried Deep* (Story Line Press, 2003, to be reissued by Tupelo Press), *Vocabulary of Silence* (Red Hen Press, 2011), and *Rootwork* (3: A Taos Press, 2015). She is the co-editor of the *Taos Journal of International Poetry & Art*, and poetry editor for the *Journal of Feminist Studies in Religion*. She lives in New Mexico with her husband, writer David Perez.

Amy Gordon is a writer of children's and young adult books, most recently *Painting the Rainbow* (Holiday House, 2014, winner of the 2015 Paterson Prize for Books for Young People), *The Shadow Collector's Apprentice* (Holiday House, 2012), and *Twenty Gold Falcons* (Holiday House, 2010). Her poetry has appeared in *The Massachusetts Review* and *The Aurorean*. She lives in Western Massachusetts.

E. A. Gordon's poems have appeared in *Painted Bride Quarterly, Indie Soleil, HIV Here & Now, The Globe and Mail,* and other publications. She grew up in Wisconsin and California and is a longtime journalist and editor. She lives in New Haven, Connecticut, and is a sound improviser for the Dirty Little Secrets Improv Show in New York City.

Arielle Greenberg's most recent books are *Come Along With Me to the Pasture Now* (Agape Editions, forthcoming 2018), the collection of micro-essays *Locally Made Panties* (Ricochet Editions, 2016), and *Slice* (Coconut Books, 2015). She has been the editor of several publications, and co-edited *Gurlesque: the new grrly, grotesque, burlesque poetics* (Saturnalia Books, 2010) with Lara Glenum. She lives in Maine, and edits and teaches in the local community and elsewhere.

Ellen Greenfield is the author of the novels *White Roses* (3Ring Press, 2017) and *Come From Nowhere* (3Ring Press, 2012). Her non-fiction books include *House Dangerous* (Vintage, 1986) and *You Can Have an Easier Delivery* (Contemporary Books, 1988). Her articles, poems, and short fiction have appeared in *Beloit Poetry Journal, Jewish Women's Literary Annual, Rosebud, Washington Square Review, Women's Wear Daily,* and other publications. She is currently a writing mentor with the Visible Ink program at Memorial Sloan Kettering Cancer Center.

Oz Hardwick is co-author, with Amina Alyal, of the Saboteur-shortlisted *Close as Second Skins* (Indigo Dreams Publishing, 2015). He is a poet, photographer, music journalist, and occasional musician based in York (UK). He is a professor of English at Leeds Trinity University, and has written extensively on misericords and animal iconography in the Middle Ages.

Walter Holland is the author of *Circuit* (Chelsea Station Editions, 2010), *Transatlantic* (Painted Leaf Press, 2001), and *A Journal of the Plague Years: Poems 1979-1992* (Magic City, 1992), as well as his novel *The March* (Chelsea Station Editions, 2011). His work has appeared in *The Antioch Review*, *Assaracus*, *HazMat Literary Review*, *Redivider*, *RHINO*, and other publications. He holds a BA from Bard, an MA from City College, and a PhD in English literature from the Graduate Center, CUNY. He lives in New York City and is a regular contributor to *Lambda Literary Review* and *Pleiades*.

Judith Hoyer is the author of *Bits and Pieces Set Aside* (Finishing Line Press, 2017). Her poems have appeared in *The Worcester Review*, *PMS poemmemoirstory*, *Spillway Magazine*, *Main Street Rag*, *Small Portions Magazine*, *Yale Journal for Humanities in Medicine*, and other publications. Before retiring she was a psychologist working in a small school district in Massachusetts.

Henry Israeli is the author of *god's breath hovering across the waters* (Four Way Books, 2016), *Praying to the Black Cat* (Del Sol, 2010), and *New Messiahs* (Four Way Books, 2002). He is the translator of *Fresco: the Selected Poetry of Luljeta Lleshanaku* (New Directions, 2002), *Child of Nature* (New Directions, 2010), and *Haywire: New and Selected Poems* (Bloodaxe, 2011). He has been awarded fellowship grants from the National Endowment for the Arts, and the Canada Council for the Arts. He is an associate professor of English at Drexel University and the founder and editor of Saturnalia Books.

Patricia Spears Jones is an African American poet, playwright, anthologist, and cultural activist. She is the author of *A Lucent Fire: New and Selected Poems* (White Pine Press, 2015), *Living in the Love Economy* (Overpass Books, 2014), and six other poetry collections. Her plays, commissioned by Mabou Mines, were presented in New York City. She is a recipient of awards from the NEA, NYFA, the NY Community Trust, and the Foundation for Contemporary Arts. She is the Poets & Writers 2017 Jackson Poetry Prize recipient, and a winner of the Pushcart Prize.

Stephanie Kaylor is based in Upstate New York and is currently an MA student in philosophy, art, and critical thought at the European Graduate School. She holds an MA in women's, gender, and sexuality studies from the University at Albany, is the managing editor for *Five:2:One Magazine*, and is the reviews editor for *Glass: A Journal of Poetry*.

Jennifer L. Knox is the author of *Days of Shame and Failure* (Bloof Books, 2015), *The Mystery of the Hidden Driveway* (Bloof Books, 2010), *Drunk by Noon* (Bloof Books, 2007), and *A Gringo Like Me* (Bloof Books 2005). Her poems have appeared four times in the *Best American Poetry* series (Simon & Schuster, 1997, 2003, 2006, 2011), as well as in the anthologies *Great American Prose Poems: From Poe to the Present* (Scribner, 2003) and *Best American Erotic Poems* (Scribner, 2008). Her work has appeared in *The New York Times*, *The New Yorker*, *American Poetry Review*, and other publications.

Joy Ladin is the author of nine books of poetry, including *The Future is Trying to Tell Us Something: New and Selected Poems* (Sheep Meadow Press, 2017), and Lambda Literary Award finalists *Impersonation* (Sheep Meadow, 2015) and *Transmigration* (Sheep Meadow, 2009). Her memoir of gender transition, *Through the Door of Life* (University of Wisconsin Press, 2012), was a 2012 National Jewish Book Award finalist. Her work has been recognized with a National Endowment of the Arts fellowship and a Fulbright Scholarship, among other honors. She holds the Gottesman Chair in English at Yeshiva University.

Jenna Le is the author of *Six Rivers* (NYQ Books, 2011) and *A History of the Cetacean American Diaspora* (Anchor & Plume, 2016). Her poems are anthologized in *The Best of the Raintown Review* (Barefoot Muse Press, 2015), *The 2016 Rhysling Anthology: The Best Science Fiction, Fantasy & Horror Poetry* (Science Fiction Poetry Association, 2016), *Two-Countries: U.S. Daughters and Sons of Immigrant Parents* (Red Hen Press, 2017), and

Nasty Women Poets: An Unapologetic Anthology of Subversive Verse (Lost Horse Press, 2017). She is a physician and a daughter of Vietnamese refugees.

Timothy Liu is the author of several poetry collections, including *Don't Go Back To Sleep* (Saturnalia Books, 2014), *Bending the Mind Around the Dream's Blown Fuse* (Talisman House, Publishers, 2009), and *For Dust Thou Art* (Southern Illinois University Press, 2005). His poems have appeared in *BOMB, Grand Street, The Kenyon Review, The Nation, The Paris Review, Ploughshares, Virginia Quarterly Review, The Yale Review*, and other publications. He was nominated for the Lambda Literary Award for Gay Men's Poetry, and is a Pushcart Prize winner. He lives in Manhattan and Woodstock, NY.

Elizabeth Macklin is the author of *You've Just Been Told* (Norton, 2000) and *A Woman Kneeling in the Big City* (Norton, 1992). She translated the Basque poet Kirmen Uribe's *Bitartean Heldu Eskutik (Meanwhile Take My Hand)* (Graywolf, 2007). Her work has appeared in *The Nation, New England Review, The New Republic, The New Yorker, The New York Times, Paris Review, The Threepenny Review, Boston Review*, and other publications. Her awards include the Ingram Merrill poetry prize, a Guggenheim Fellowship in Poetry, the Amy Lowell Poetry Travelling Scholarship, and a PEN Translation Fund Grant from PEN American Center.

Ed Madden's most recent book is *Ark* (Sibling Rivalry Press, 2016), a memoir in poems about returning to Arkansas to help with his father's home hospice care in his last months with cancer. He is also the author of *Nest* (Salmon Publishing, 2014), *Prodigal: Variations* (Lethe Press, 2011), and *Signals* (USC, 2008). He is a professor of English and director of the Women's & Gender Studies Program at the University of South Carolina. He is the poet laureate for Columbia, SC.

Lucinda Marshall is an award-winning writer, an artist and activist. Her poems have appeared recently in *Sediments, One Sentence*

Poems, Stepping Stones Magazine, Columbia Journal, Poetica Magazine, Haikuniverse, and *ISLE.* Her poem "The Lilies Were In Bloom" received an honorable mention in Waterline Writers' "Artists as Visionaries: Climate Crisis Solutions" galley exhibition in Batavia, Illinois. The author of numerous essays and articles, she blogs at *Reclaiming Medusa.* She mentors the award-winning Gaithersburg, MD Teen Writing Club, and hosts the DiVerse poetry reading and open mic series in Gaithersburg.

Kristi Maxwell is the author of *Plan/k* (Horse Less Press, 2015), *That Our Eyes Be Rigged* (Saturnalia Books, 2014), RE- (Ahsahta Press, 2011), *Hush Sessions* (Saturnalia Books, 2009), and *Realm Sixty-Four* (Ahsahta Press, 2008). Her honors include the Greta Wrolstad Scholarship for Young Poets through the Summer Literary Seminars, the Phyllis Smart-Young Prize in Poetry, and the Margaret Sterling Memorial Award.

Laura McCullough is the author of *The Wild Night Dress* (University of Arkansas Press, 2017), selected by Billy Collins in the Miller Williams Poetry Prize Series. Her other books of poetry include *Jersey Mercy* (Black Lawrence Press, 2016), *Rigger Death & Hoist Another* (Black Lawrence Press, 2013), and *Panic* (Alice James Books, 2011), among others. She curated two anthologies of essays on poetry, *A Sense of Regard: Essays on Poetry and Race* (University of Georgia Press, 2015) and *The Room and the World: Essays on the Poet Stephen Dunn* (University of Syracuse Press, 2013). Her work has appeared in *Michigan Quarterly Review, The Southern Review, The Georgia Review, The American Poetry Review, Guernica, PANK, Gulf Coast, The Writer's Chronicle, Best American Poetry,* and other publications. She teaches full time at Brookdale Community College in NJ, and is on the faculty of the Sierra Nevada low-res MFA. She is the founding editor of *Mead: the Magazine of Literature and Libations.*

Noah Mendez's work has appeared in *The Rising Phoenix Review, HIV Here & Now, Brouhaha Magazine, Thank You For Swallowing, Three Drops from a Cauldron,* and other journals, as well as the anthology *Defining Myself: Transmasculine Experience Through Poetry* (Boundless Endeavors, 2016). He has performed at Urban Word and the Apollo Theater. He is an eighteen-year-old Hispanic, mentally ill, trans man who is utterly terrified for the fate of this nation.

Day Merrill's poems have appeared or are forthcoming in *Tin Roof Press, Halcyon, The Binnacle, Contemporary Rural Social Work, HIV Here & Now,* and *Quick Brown Fox.* After a career as an English teacher and a university administrator, she became a career coach. A dual US/Canadian citizen, she lives in Collingwood, Ontario, on the shores of Georgian Bay/Lake Huron with her husband and a rescued dog and cat.

Sharon Mesmer is the author of *Greetings From My Girlie Leisure Place* (Bloof Books, 2015), voted "Best of 2015" by *Entropy.* Previous poetry collections are *Annoying Diabetic Bitch* (Combo Books, 2008), *The Virgin Formica* (Hanging Loose Press, 2008), *Vertigo Seeks Affinities* (Belladonna Books, 2007), and *Half Angel, Half Lunch* (Hard Press, 1998). Four of her poems appeared in *Postmodern American Poetry: A Norton Anthology* (second edition, 2013). Her fiction collections are *Ma Vie à Yonago* (Hachette Littératures, Paris, in French translation, 2005), *In Ordinary Time* (Hanging Loose Press, 2005), and *The Empty Quarter* (Hanging Loose Press, 2000). Her essays, reviews, and interviews have appeared in *The New York Times, Paris Review, American Poetry Review,* and *The Brooklyn Rail,* among other publications. She lives in Brooklyn, and teaches in the undergraduate and graduate programs of New York University and The New School.

Leah Mueller is author of *Beach Dweller's Manifesto* (Writing Knights Press, 2017), *Allergic to Everything* (Writing Knights Press, 2015), and *The Underside of the Snake* (Red Ferret Press, 2015), as well as the chapbooks *Political Apnea* (Locofo Chaps, 2017) and *Queen of Dorksville* (Crisis Chronicles Press, 2012). Her work has appeared in *Blunderbuss Magazine, Memoryhouse Magazine, Atticus Review,* and other publications. She was a runner-up in the 2012 Wergle Flomp Humor Poetry Contest, and a featured poet at the 2015 New York Poetry Festival.

Peter E. Murphy is the author of *Stubborn Child* (Jane Street Press, 2005, finalist for the Paterson Poetry Prize), *Challenges for the Delusional*

(Jane Street Press, 2012), and five poetry chapbooks. His work appears in *The Common, Diode, Guernica, Hawaii Pacific Review, The New Welsh Reader, The Atlanta Review, New York Quarterly, Rattle, Word Riot,* and other publications. He is the founder of Murphy Writing of Stockton University.

Sergio Ortiz, a gay Puerto Rican poet, is the founding editor of *Undertow Tanka Review*. His collections of tanka poetry include *For the Men to Come* (2014) and *From Life to Life* (2014), both released by Amazon, as well as *Bedbugs in My Mattress* (Flutter Press, 2010), and *At the Tail End of Dusk* (Flutter Press, 2009). His work has appeared in *Moko Magazine, *82 review, Crab Fat Magazine, Gramma Poetry, FLAME! GLBTQ+ Arts & Literary Magazine*, and other publications.

W. P. Osborn is the author of *Seven Tales and Seven Stories* (Unboxed Books, 2013), which won the 2013 Unboxed Books Prize in Fiction, selected by Francine Prose. His short work has appeared in *Chicago Quarterly Review, Southern Humanities Review, Texas Review, Hotel Amerika, Mississippi Review, Gettysburg Review, Beloit Fiction Journal, Gargoyle,* and other publications.

Ina Roy-Faderman's poems have appeared in *Right Hand Pointing*, the Tupelo 30/30 project, *HIV Here & Now*, and other publications. She is the co-editor of *56 Days of August*, an anthology of postcard poetry and art (Five Oaks Press, 2017). Recognitions in 2017 include *Richmond Anthology of Poetry* Best Poem (Norfolk Press, 2016) and a Pushcart nomination for fiction. Educated at Stanford (MD) and U.C. Berkeley (PhD), she teaches university bioethics, works as the librarian at a school for gifted children, and is an assistant fiction editor for *Rivet Magazine*.

Sarah Sarai is the author of *Geographies of Soul and Taffeta* (Indolent Books, 2016) and *The Future Is Happy* (BlazeVOX Books, 2009). Her poetry has appeared in *Barrow Street, Boston Review, The Collagist, Prelude,* and other journals, as well as the anthologies *Composing Poetry, a Guide to Writing Poems and Thinking Lyrically* (Kendall Hunt Publishing,

2016), *Gathered: Contemporary Quaker Poetry* (Sundress Publications, 2013), *Say It Loud: Poems About James Brown* (Whirlwind Press, 2011), and *The OR Panthology: Ocellus Reseau* (Other Rooms Press, 2013).

Lynn Schmeidler's poems have appeared or are forthcoming in *The Awl, Barrow Street, Boston Review, Fence,* and other journals, as well as in several anthologies including *Drawn to Marvel: Poems from the Comic Books* (Minor Arcana Press, 2014), *Bared* (Les Femmes Folles Books, 2014), and *Nasty Women Poets: An Unapologetic Anthology of Subversive Verse* (Lost Horse Press, 2017). She is the author of the chapbooks *Curiouser & Curiouser* (Grayson Books, 2013, winner of the 2013 Grayson Books Chapbook Contest) and *Wrack Lines* (Grayson Books, 2017), as well as the full-length collection *History of Gone* (Veliz Books, 2018).

Pat Schneider's most recent book is *How the Light Gets In: Writing as a Spiritual Practice* (Oxford University Press, 2013). Her work has appeared in *Chrysalis, Deus Loci: The Lawrence Durrell Journal, Minnesota Review, Ms., New York Quarterly, North Dakota Quarterly, Sewanee Review, The Sun, Thema,* and other publications. She is the founder of Amherst Writers & Artists, an international network of workshop leaders who use the writing method described in her book, *Writing Alone and With Others* (Oxford University Press, 2003). For her work with under-served populations, she has received grants from the National Endowment for the Arts and the Massachusetts Cultural Council.

Jason Schneiderman is the author of *Primary Source* (Red Hen Press, 2016), *Striking Surface* (Ashland Poetry Press, 2010), and *Sublimation Point* (Four Way Books, 2004). He edited the anthology *Queer: A Reader for Writers* (Oxford University Press, 2015). His work has appeared in journals and anthologies including *American Poetry Review, The Best American Poetry* (Simon & Schuster, 2004), *Poetry London, Grand Street, The Penguin Book of the Sonnet* (Penguin Books, 2001), *StoryQuarterly,* and *Tin House.* He is the poetry editor of the *Bellevue Literary Review* and associate editor of *Painted Bride Quarterly.* He's an associate professor of English at the Borough of Manhattan Community College, CUNY.

Elaine Sexton is the author of *Prospect/Refuge* (Sheep Meadow, 2015), *Causeway* (New Issues Press, 2008), and *Sleuth* (New Issues Press, 2003). A poet, critic, and teacher, her work appears in the election-related anthology *Nasty Women Poets: An Unapologetic Anthology of Subversive Verse* (Lost Horse Press, 2017).

Hilary Sideris is the author of *The Inclination to Make Waves* (Big Wonderful, 2016), and *Most Likely to Die* (Poets Wear Prada, 2014), which features poems in the voice of Keith Richards. Her new chapbook, A *House Not Made with Hands*, inspired by Vasari's *Lives of the Artists*, is forthcoming from Poets Wear Prada. She lives in Kensington, Brooklyn.

Suzanne Sigafoos is the author of *Held In The Weave* (Finishing Line Press, 2011). Her work has appeared in *The Oregonian*, *VoiceCatcher*, *Bellingham Review*, and *Windfall: A Journal of Poetry of Place*, and in the anthology *The Knotted Bond: Oregon Poets Speak of their Sisters* (Uttered Chaos, 2014). She lives in Portland, Oregon.

Sarah Dickenson Snyder is the author of *The Human Contract* (Aldrich Press, 2017) and *Notes from a Nomad* (Finishing Line Press, 2017). Her work has appeared or is forthcoming in *Chautauqua*, *Piedmont Journal*, *Sunlight Press*, *The Comstock Review*, *Main Street Rag*, *Passager*, *immix*, *Whale Road Review*, *Stirring: A Literary Collection*, *Eyedrum Periodically*, and *Panoplyzine*. One of her poems was recently selected by the Mass Poetry Festival Migration Contest 2017 to be stenciled on the sidewalk in Salem, MA. She has received several awards from the Poetry Society of Vermont, and in 2016 she was selected for Tupelo Press's "30/30 Project".

Darius Stewart is the author of *The Terribly Beautiful* (Main Street Rag Publishing Company, 2006) and *Sotto Voce* (Main Street Rag, 2008), each an Editor's Choice Selection in the Main Street Rag Poetry Chapbook Series. His third chapbook, *The Ghost the Night Becomes* (Gertrude Press, 2014), won the 2013 Gertrude Press Poetry Chapbook Prize. Other poems and prose appear in various literary journals and anthologies. He is a former James A. Michener Fellow in poetry, and received his MFA from the University of Texas at Austin. Currently, he is a first-year MFA candidate in the nonfiction writing program at the University of Iowa, where he also teaches "The Interpretation of Literature". He lives in Iowa City, Iowa with his dog, Fry.

Christine Stoddard is the author of several books, including *Ova* (dancing girl press, 2017), *Hispanic & Latino Heritage in Virginia* (The History Press, 2016), and two miniature books from the Poems-For-All series. Her work has appeared in *Marie Claire, The Feminist Wire, Bustle, Teen Vogue, The Huffington Post, Ravishly, So to Speak*, and other publications. She is a Salvadoran-Scottish-American writer and artist who lives in Brooklyn, and the founding editor of *Quail Bell Magazine*.

Mary Ellen Talley's poems have most recently appeared in *Typoetic. us* and *Kaleidoscope*, as well as in the anthologies *The Doll Collection* (Terrapin Books, 2016), *All We Can Hold: poems of motherhood* (Sage Hill Press, 2016), and *Raising Lilly Ledbetter: Women Poets Occupy the Workspace* (Lost Horse Press, 2015). She is a Pushcart Prize nominee. She has worked for many years with words and children as a speech-language pathologist in public schools in Washington.

Cammy Thomas has written two collections of poetry, *Inscriptions* (Four Way Books, 2014) and *Cathedral of Wish* (Four Way Books, 2006, winner of the 2006 Norma Farber First Book Award from the Poetry Society of America). Her poems are published or forthcoming in *The Missouri Review, Salamander, Ibbetson Street Press, The Maine Review*, and *Off the Coast*. She lives in Lexington, Massachusetts.

Sarah Van Arsdale is the author of a collection of novellas titled *In Case of Emergency, Break Glass* (Queen's Ferry Press, 2016), and the long narrative poem *The Catamount* (Nomadic Press, 2017), both illustrated with her watercolors. Her novels are *Grand Isle* (SUNY Press, 2012), *Blue* (University of Tennessee Press, 2003, winner of the Peter Taylor Prize for the Novel), and *Toward Amnesia* (Riverhead Books, 1996). She serves on the board of the Ferro-Grumley Award in LGBTQ Fiction, and teaches in the Antioch University MFA program and at NYU.

Emily Vieweg is the author of *Look Where She Points* (Plan B Press, 2017). Her work has appeared in *Foliate Oak Literary Magazine, The Voices Project, Red Weather, Soundings Review, Art Young's Good Morning,* and other publications. She is a poet and educator originally from St. Louis, Missouri. She now lives in Fargo, North Dakota with her two children.

Lynne Viti is the author of *Baltimore Girls* (Finishing Line Press, 2017). Her work has appeared in *The South Florida Poetry Journal, Little Patuxent Review, Mountain Gazette, Amuse-Bouche, The Paterson Review, Drunk Monkeys, Cultured Vultures,* and other publications. She teaches in the writing program at Wellesley College.

Julie Marie Wade is the author of eight collections of poetry and prose, including *SIX* (Red Hen Press, 2016, winner of AROHO's 2014 To the Lighthouse Poetry Prize), *Catechism: A Love Story* (Noctuary Press, 2016), and *When I Was Straight* (A Midsummer Night's Press, 2014). Her work has appeared in *Tupelo Quarterly, PANK, Bellingham Review, TriQuarterly, Seneca Review,* and other publications. She teaches in the creative writing program at Florida International University and reviews regularly for *Lambda Literary Review* and *The Rumpus*. She is married to Angie Griffin and lives on Hollywood Beach.

Vivian Wagner is the author of the memoir *Fiddle: One Woman, Four Strings, and 8,000 Miles of Music* (Citadel-Kensington, 2010) and the poetry chapbook *The Village* (Kelsay Books, 2017). Her work has appeared in *McSweeney's Internet Tendency, Creative Nonfiction, The Atlantic, The Ilanot Review, Silk Road Review, Zone 3,* and other publications. She is an associate professor of English at Muskingum University in New Concord, Ohio.

Francisco-Luis White is an agender Afro-Latinx poet, storyteller and advocate, and author of the poetry chapbook *Found Them* (Createspace

Independent Publishing Platform, 2016). They have presented at the Fire & Ink: Witness Conference for LGBTQ writers of African descent, Carolina Conference on Queer Youth, the United States Conference on AIDS, and was a keynote speaker at the 2017 Northeast Queer and Trans People of Color Conference. They have been recognized by National Black Justice Coalition as an LGBTQ Emerging Leader to Watch. Their first full poetry collection is forthcoming from Indolent Books in 2018.

Scott Wiggerman is the author of *Leaf and Beak: Sonnets* (purple flag, 2015), *Presence* (Pecan Grove Press, 2011), and *Vegetables and Other Relationships* (Plain View Press, 2000). He is the editor of several volumes, including *Wingbeats: Exercises & Practice in Poetry* (Dos Gatos Press, 2011), *Lifting the Sky: Southwestern Haiku & Haiga* (Dos Gatos Press, 2013), and *Bearing the Mask* (Dos Gatos Press, 2016). His poems have appeared in *A Quiet Courage, Naugatuck River Review, Red Earth Review, Rat's Ass Review, shufPoetry, Yellow Chair Review*, and other publications. He lives with his husband, the writer David Meischen, in Albuquerque, NM.

Laura Winberry is the author of *bell lap* (Indolent Books, 2018). Her collaborations with the poet Emily Carr have appeared in *Hermeneutic Chaos Journal* and *Contemporary Verse 2*. She is an Oregon State University-Cascades low-res MFA alumna and a professional cyclocross racer. She has written articles for *Patagonia* and *Speedbloggen*, co-runs the blog *(Eternal) Beginner's Guide to Bend* with Irene Cooper, and is a curator at *The Stay Project*.

ABOUT THE EDITOR

Michael Broder is the author of *Drug and Disease Free* (Indolent Books, 2016) and *This Life Now* (A Midsummer Night's Press, 2014), a finalist for the 2015 Lambda Literary Award for Gay Poetry. His poems have appeared in *American Poetry Review*, *Assaracus*, *BLOOM*, *Columbia Poetry Review*, *Court Green*, *OCHO*, *Painted Bride Quarterly*, and other journals, as well as in the anthologies *This New Breed: Gents, Bad Boys and Barbarians 2* (Windstorm Creative, 2004), edited by Rudy Kikel; *My Diva: 65 Gay Men on the Women Who Inspire Them* (Terrace Books, 2009), edited by Michael Montlack; *Spaces Between Us: Poetry, Prose and Art on HIV/AIDS* (Third World Press, 2010), edited by Kelly Norman Ellis and ML Hunter; *Divining Divas: 50 Gay Men on Their Muses* (Lethe Press, 2012), edited by Michael Montlack; and *Multilingual Anthology: The Americas Poetry Festival of New York 2015* (Artepoética Press, 2015), edited by Carlos Aguasaco and Yrene Santos. He lives in Brooklyn with his husband, the poet Jason Schneiderman, and a backyard colony of stray and feral cats.

ABOUT INDOLENT BOOKS

Indolent Books is a small nonprofit poetry press founded in 2015 and operating in Brooklyn, N.Y. Indolent was founded as a home for poets of a certain age who have not published a first collection. But the mission of the press is broader than that: Ultimately, Indolent publishes books we care about. The main criteria are that the work be innovative, provocative, risky, and relevant. Indolent is queer flavored but inclusive and maintains a commitment to diversity among authors, artists, designers, developers, and other team members. Indolent Books is an imprint of Indolent Arts Foundation, Inc., a 501(c)(3) nonprofit charity founded in January 2017.

www.ingramcontent.com/pod-product-compliance
Lightning Source LLC
Chambersburg PA
CBHW021439080526
44588CB00009B/607